ABOUT THIS WORKBOOK

This workbook was designed to facilitate English Language Learners (ELLs) in their language development. The importance of practice and application is the foundation for this resource. It is important that English Language Learners are given the guidance, support, and opportunities to practice language learning in familiar and academic context.

The workbook activities coincide with the California English Language Development Standards. Educators can track and record their students' progression and acquisition of the English language.

Guided activities provide both educators and ELLs with appropriate levels of support. The activities expose the students to the format and language expectations of the English Language Proficiency Assessment for California (ELPAC). Similar to a test prep manual, this workbook will help familiarize ELLs with the ELPAC. However, this workbook can be a great resource to ALL language learners and doesn't have to be limited to just EL students.

The practice activities are another added layer of support for ELLs. The expected outcome of English language acquisition can be complemented with this great resource!

OTHER ELPAC RESOURCES AVAILABLE:

KINDERGARTEN
SPEAKING

LISTENING

READING

WRITING

FIRST GRADE
SPEAKING

LISTENING

READING

WRITING

SECOND GRADE
SPEAKING

LISTENING

WRITING

THIRD-FIFTH GRADE
SPEAKING

LISTENING

READING

WRITING

Table of Contents

Reading

Read and Choose a Word

- Section Directions 1
- Guided Activities 2
- ELD Standards & Recording Sheets 13
- Practice Activities 15

Read and Choose a Sentence

- Section Directions 20
- Guided Activities 21
- ELD Standards & Recording Sheets 31
- Practice Activities 33

Read a Short Informational Passage

- Section Directions 38
- Guided Activities 39
- ELD Standards & Recording Sheets 54
- Practice Activities 56

Read a Literary Passage

- Section Directions 66
- Guided Activities 68
- ELD Standards & Recording Sheets 83
- Practice Activities 91

Read an Informational Passage

- Section Directions 101
- Guided Activities 103
- ELD Standards & Recording Sheets 118
- Practice Activities 126

Reading
Read and Choose a Word

This section includes:
- Guided Activities
- Teacher's ELD Standards Record Sheet
- Student Practice Activities:
  - Word Practice and Picture Matchup
  - Using the word in a complete sentence

- -

Alignment to CA ELD Standards:

Alignment to CCSS:

Part I: Interacting in Meaningful Ways

<u>B.6 Reading/viewing closely</u>
Reading closely literary and informational texts and viewing multimedia to determine how meaning is conveyed explicitly and implicitly through language

RL.2.1–7, 9–10; RI.2.1–7, 9–10; SL.2.2–3; L.2.3, 4, 6

- -

Guided Activities Direction:
1. Show students the picture.
2. Follow the teacher directions.
3. **Say** the **Teacher Script** (indicated by)
4. Guide students through:
   - Identifying and matching pictures to the correct word
   - Independently reading the words.
5. Then have students match the picture to one of three words.

Guided Activity Words List

List #1

tray

book

sleep

barn

List #2

house

grow

kick

trip

List #3

dig

wish

swim

crab

List #4

fall

bear

step

plant

List #5

dance

yawn

laugh

heat

Guided Activity #1

1

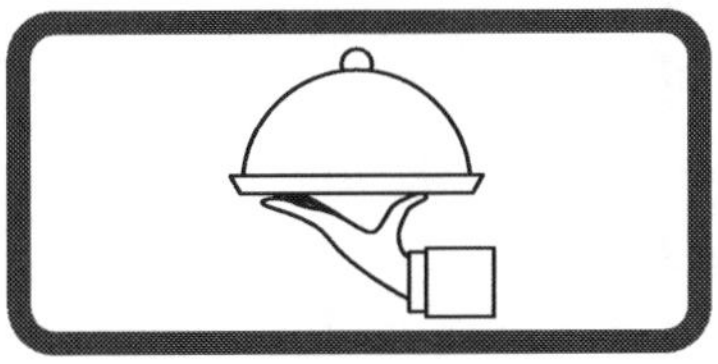

A run

B blink

C tray

2

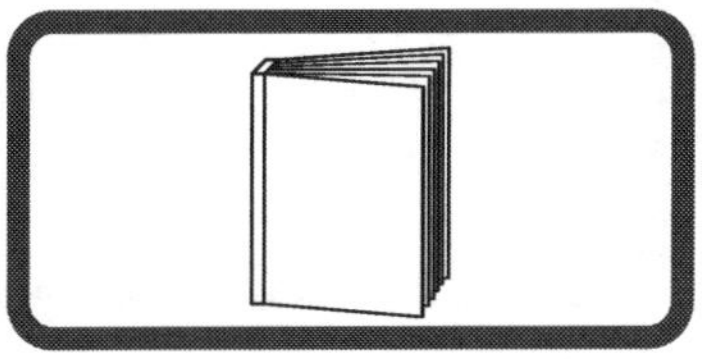

A map

B book

C stand

3

A sleep

B trip

C couch

4

A far

B barn

C crops

Guided Activity #1

1

A run

B blink

C tray

SAY Point to the picture.
Look at the picture.
Choose the word that matches the picture.

2

A map

B book

C stand

SAY Point to the picture.
Look at the picture.
Choose the word that matches the picture.

3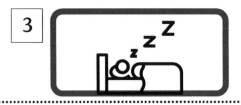

A sleep

B trip

C couch

SAY Point to the picture.
Look at the picture.
Choose the word that matches the picture.

4

A far

B barn

C crops

SAY Point to the picture.
Look at the picture.
Choose the word that matches the picture.

Reading: *Read and Choose a Word*

Guided Activity #2

1

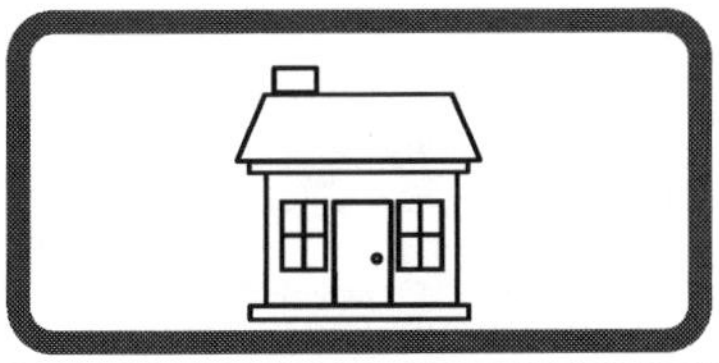

A farm

B huge

C house

2

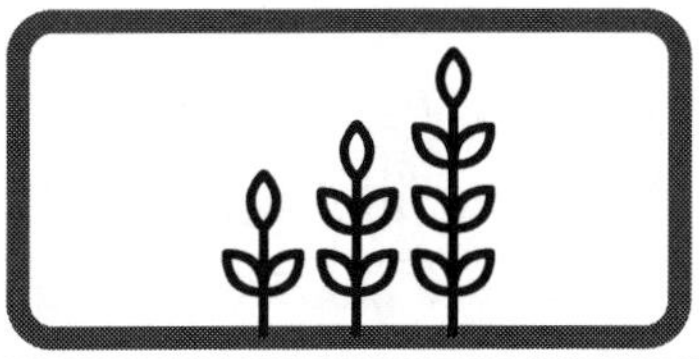

A grow

B vent

C jump

3

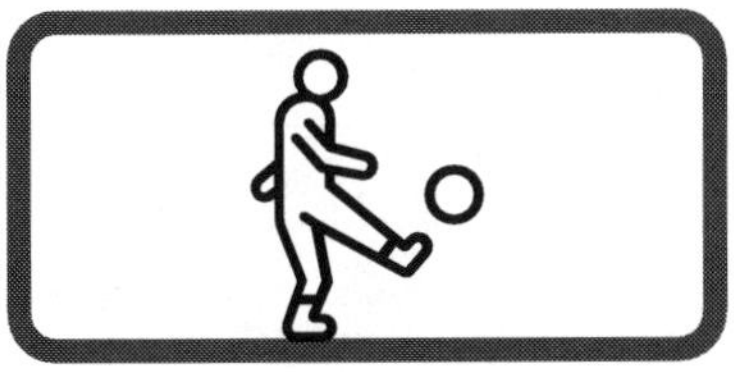

A hole

B kick

C pluck

4

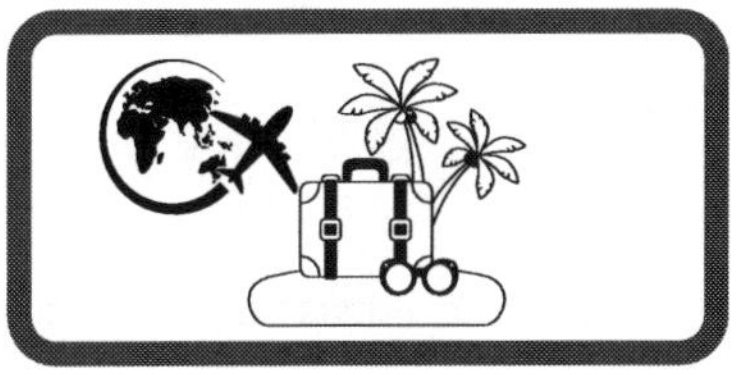

A trip

B yard

C quit

Guided Activity #2

1

....

- A farm
- B huge
- C house

SAY Point to the picture.
Look at the picture.
Choose the word that matches the picture.

2

....

- A grow
- B vent
- C jump

SAY Point to the picture.
Look at the picture.
Choose the word that matches the picture.

3

....

- A hole
- B kick
- C pluck

SAY Point to the picture.
Look at the picture.
Choose the word that matches the picture.

4

....

- A trip
- B yard
- C quit

SAY Point to the picture.
Look at the picture.
Choose the word that matches the picture.

6

Guided Activity #3

1
- A dig
- B grip
- C bend

2
- A wish
- B love
- C new

3
- A ride
- B swim
- C from

4
- A chop
- B park
- C crab

Guided Activity #3

1

A dig

B grip

C bend

SAY Point to the picture.
Look at the picture.
Choose the word that matches the picture.

2

A wish

B love

C new

SAY Point to the picture.
Look at the picture.
Choose the word that matches the picture.

3

A ride

B swim

C from

SAY Point to the picture.
Look at the picture.
Choose the word that matches the picture.

4

A chop

B park

C crab

SAY Point to the picture.
Look at the picture.
Choose the word that matches the picture.

Reading: *Read and Choose a Word*

Guided Activity #4

1

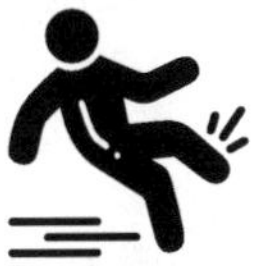

A dark

B fall

C slap

2

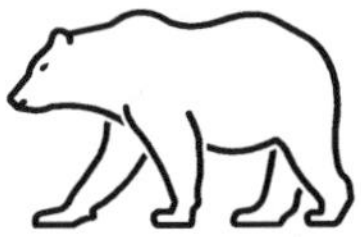

A bear

B drive

C joke

3

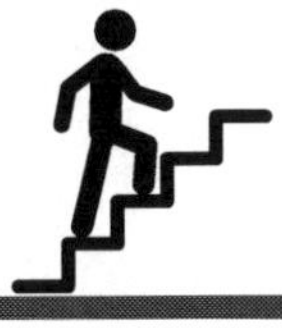

A step

B went

C you

4

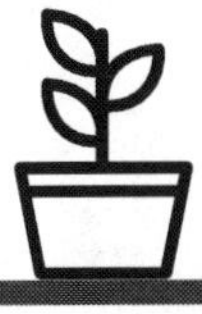

A kind

B cord

C plant

Guided Activity #4

1

A dark

B fall

C slap

SAY Point to the picture.
Look at the picture.
Choose the word that matches the
picture.

2

A bear

B drive

C joke

SAY Point to the picture.
Look at the picture.
Choose the word that matches the
picture.

3

A step

B went

C you

SAY Point to the picture.
Look at the picture.
Choose the word that matches the
picture.

4

A kind

B cord

C plant

SAY Point to the picture.
Look at the picture.
Choose the word that matches the
picture.

Reading: *Read and Choose a Word*

Guided Activity #5

1 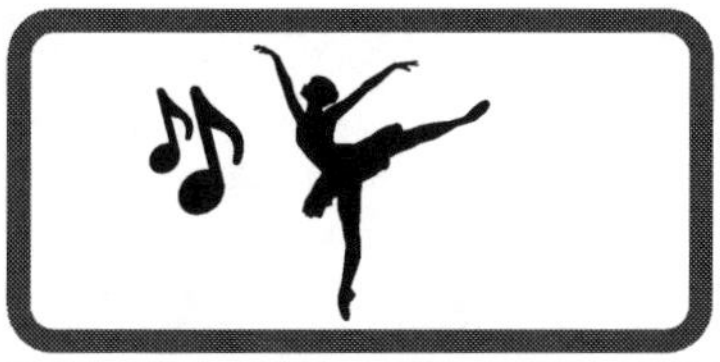

A kid

B dance

C mop

2 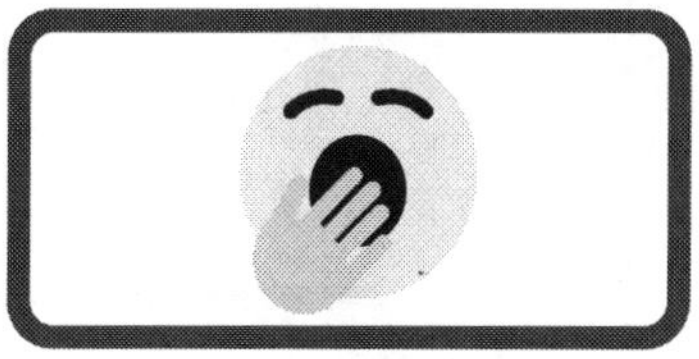

A find

B love

C yawn

3 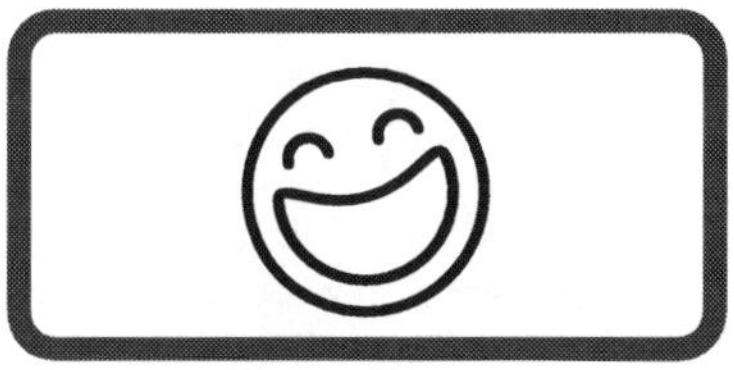

A laugh

B brag

C pump

4 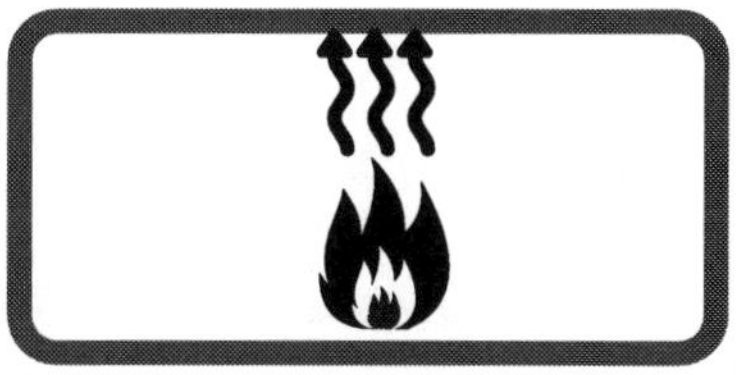

A hug

B heat

C know

Guided Activity #5

1

⬛A kid

⬛B dance

⬛C mop

SAY Point to the picture.
Look at the picture.
Choose the word that matches the picture.

2

⬛A find

⬛B love

⬛C yawn

SAY Point to the picture.
Look at the picture.
Choose the word that matches the picture.

3

⬛A laugh

⬛B brag

⬛C pump

SAY Point to the picture.
Look at the picture.
Choose the word that matches the picture.

4

⬛A hug

⬛B heat

⬛C know

SAY Point to the picture.
Look at the picture.
Choose the word that matches the picture.

ELD Standards Record Sheet

Directions:

1. Look at the CA ELD standards (**BELOW**) that correspond to this section.
2. Reference these specific standards for the template Record Sheet.
3. Use the following template Record Sheet to monitor students' proficiency levels for the **GUIDED ACTIVITIES** in this section.
4. Fill out all the information. Circle, check, highlight the proficiency level. (*There is space for 20 students. Make additional copies, as needed*)
5. Retain for your records to be used during grading, parent/student conferences, lesson planning, ELD documentation, etc.

 Suggestion: You can make one copy of each guided activity and/or the student practice sheets and laminate them. Organize the laminated sheets onto a book ring. Now it'll be easily accessible for whole group, small group, one-on-one, centers, etc. Copy as many of the ELD Standards Record Sheet as you need and keep it handy along with the activities.

CA ELD Standards & Proficiency Levels
Part I: Interacting in Meaningful Ways
B.6 Reading/viewing closely

EMERGING (EM)	EXPANDING (EX)	BRIDGING (BR)
*Requires **Substantial** Support*	*Requires **Moderate** Support*	*Requires **Light** Support*

• Describes:
  ○ Ideas
  ○ phenomena (e.g., plant life cycle)
  ○ text elements (e.g. main idea,
• characters, events)
• Reads and comprehends a select set of grade-level texts and multimedia with:
  ○ Simple sentences
  ○ Familiar vocabulary
  ○ Support by graphics or pictures
• Requires substantial support
	• Describes in <u>greater details</u>:
	  ○ Ideas
	  ○ phenomena (e.g., how earthworms eat)
	  ○ text elements (e.g. setting, events)
	• Reads and comprehends a <u>variety of</u> grade-level texts and multimedia with:
	  ○ <u>Reliance on content and prior</u>
	• <u>knowledge to obtain meaning from print</u>
	  ○ Support by graphics or pictures
	• Requires <u>moderate</u> support
		• Describes <u>using key details</u>:
		  ○ Ideas
		  ○ phenomena (e.g., erosion)
		  ○ text elements (e.g. central message, character traits)
		• Reads and comprehends a variety of grade-level texts and multimedia with:
		  ○ <u>Limited comprehension difficulty</u>
		  ○ <u>Comprehension of concrete and abstract topics</u>
		  ○ <u>Recognize language subtleties</u>
		  ○ Support by graphics or pictures
		• Requires <u>light</u> support

ELD Standards Record Sheet

Teacher: _____ **Class:** _____

Standards: *PI.B.6*

Guided Activities and Proficiency Levels:

Students:	#1	#2	#3	#4	#5
	EM / EX / BR	EM / EX / BR	EM / EX / BR	EM / EX / BR	EM / EX / BR
	EM / EX / BR	EM / EX / BR	EM / EX / BR	EM / EX / BR	EM / EX / BR
	EM / EX / BR	EM / EX / BR	EM / EX / BR	EM / EX / BR	EM / EX / BR
	EM / EX / BR	EM / EX / BR	EM / EX / BR	EM / EX / BR	EM / EX / BR
	EM / EX / BR	EM / EX / BR	EM / EX / BR	EM / EX / BR	EM / EX / BR
	EM / EX / BR	EM / EX / BR	EM / EX / BR	EM / EX / BR	EM / EX / BR
	EM / EX / BR	EM / EX / BR	EM / EX / BR	EM / EX / BR	EM / EX / BR
	EM / EX / BR	EM / EX / BR	EM / EX / BR	EM / EX / BR	EM / EX / BR
	EM / EX / BR	EM / EX / BR	EM / EX / BR	EM / EX / BR	EM / EX / BR
	EM / EX / BR	EM / EX / BR	EM / EX / BR	EM / EX / BR	EM / EX / BR
	EM / EX / BR	EM / EX / BR	EM / EX / BR	EM / EX / BR	EM / EX / BR
	EM / EX / BR	EM / EX / BR	EM / EX / BR	EM / EX / BR	EM / EX / BR
	EM / EX / BR	EM / EX / BR	EM / EX / BR	EM / EX / BR	EM / EX / BR
	EM / EX / BR	EM / EX / BR	EM / EX / BR	EM / EX / BR	EM / EX / BR
	EM / EX / BR	EM / EX / BR	EM / EX / BR	EM / EX / BR	EM / EX / BR
	EM / EX / BR	EM / EX / BR	EM / EX / BR	EM / EX / BR	EM / EX / BR
	EM / EX / BR	EM / EX / BR	EM / EX / BR	EM / EX / BR	EM / EX / BR
	EM / EX / BR	EM / EX / BR	EM / EX / BR	EM / EX / BR	EM / EX / BR
	EM / EX / BR	EM / EX / BR	EM / EX / BR	EM / EX / BR	EM / EX / BR

Practice Activity #1

Name:

Directions: Read the word. Trace and write the word.

move

Directions: Draw a line to match the picture to the word.

example: car

move

Directions: Use the word in a complete sentence.

Directions: Read the word. Trace and write the word.

drink

Directions: Draw a line to match the picture to the word.

example: car

drink

Directions: Use the word in a complete sentence.

Practice Activity #2

Name: ....

Directions: Read the word. Trace and write the word.

break

break

Directions: Draw a line to match the picture to the word.

example: car ··························

break

Directions: Use the word in a complete sentence.

Directions: Read the word. Trace and write the word.

ride

ride

Directions: Draw a line to match the picture to the word.

example: car ··························

ride

Directions: Use the word in a complete sentence.

Practice Activity #3

Name: ....

Directions: Read the word. Trace and write the word.

phone

Directions: Draw a line to match the picture to the word.

example: car................................

phone

Directions: Use the word in a complete sentence.

Directions: Read the word. Trace and write the word.

map

Directions: Draw a line to match the picture to the word.

example: car................................

map

Directions: Use the word in a complete sentence.

Practice Activity #4

Name: ....

Directions: Read the word. Trace and write the word.

spin

spin

Directions: Draw a line to match the picture to the word.

example: car ....

spin

Directions: Use the word in a complete sentence.

....

Directions: Read the word. Trace and write the word.

stir

stir

Directions: Draw a line to match the picture to the word.

example: car ....

stir

Directions: Use the word in a complete sentence.

....

Practice Activity #5

Name:

Directions: Read the word. Trace and write the word.

wheel

Directions: Draw a line to match the picture to the word.

example: car

wheel

Directions: Use the word in a complete sentence.

Directions: Read the word. Trace and write the word.

clock

Directions: Draw a line to match the picture to the word.

example: car

clock

Directions: Use the word in a complete sentence.

Reading
Read and Choose a Sentence

This section includes:
- Guided Activities
- Teacher's ELD Standards Record Sheet
- Student Practice Activities:
  - Picture and sentences matchup
  - Adding more details sentence writing

- -

Alignment to CA ELD Standards:

Alignment to CCSS:

Part I: Interacting in Meaningful Ways

<u>B.6 Reading/viewing closely</u>
Reading closely literary and informational texts and viewing multimedia to determine how meaning is conveyed explicitly and implicitly through language

RL.2.1–7, 9–10; RI.2.1–7, 9–10; SL.2.2–3; L.2.3, 4, 6

- -

Guided Activities Direction:
1. Show students the picture.
2. Follow the teacher directions.
3. **Say** the **Teacher Script** (indicated by)
4. Guide students through:
   - Identifying and matching pictures to the correct sentence
   - Independently reading sentences.
5. Then have students match the picture to one of three sentences.

Guided Activity #1

1

A The baby is happy.

B The baby are crying.

C The baby is crying.

. . . .

2

A A cat are taking a nap.

B A cat is taking a nap.

C A cat is thinking about food.

. . . .

3

A They are playing jump rope.

B They is playing jump rope.

C They are jump rope.

Guided Activity #1

1

A The baby is happy.

B The baby are crying.

C The baby is crying.

 Point to the picture.
Look at the picture.
Point to the sentence that matches the picture.

2

A A cat are taking a nap.

B A cat is taking a nap.

C A cat is thinking about food.

 Point to the picture.
Look at the picture.
Point to the sentence that matches the picture.

3

A They are playing jump rope.

B They is playing jump rope.

C They are jump rope.

 Point to the picture.
Look at the picture.
Point to the sentence that matches the picture.

Guided Activity #2

1

A The ship is going over the bridge.

B The ships are going under.

C The ship is going under the bridge.

2

A The wind blew the tree over.

B The winds blew the trees.

C The wind are blowing the tree.

3

A The cows is eating the grass.

B The cow is eating the grass.

C The cow and the grass.

Guided Activity #2

1

A The ship is going over the bridge.

B The ships are going under.

C The ship is going under the bridge.

SAY Point to the picture.
Look at the picture.
Point to the sentence that matches the picture.

2

A The wind blew the tree over.

B The winds blew the trees.

C The wind are blowing the tree.

SAY Point to the picture.
Look at the picture.
Point to the sentence that matches the picture.

3

A The cows is eating the grass.

B The cow is eating the grass.

C The cow and the grass.

SAY Point to the picture.
Look at the picture.
Point to the sentence that matches the picture.

Guided Activity #3

1

A The man is swimming under water.

B The man is swim under the water.

C The man swimming.

2

A The ducks is in the water.

B The duck is in the water.

C The duck are in the water.

3

A The dog is sleeping.

B The dog are barking.

C The dog is barking.

Guided Activity #3

1

A The man is swimming under water.

B The man is swim under the water.

C The man swimming.

SAY Point to the picture.
Look at the picture.
Point to the sentence that matches the picture.

2

A The ducks is in the water.

B The duck is in the water.

C The duck are in the water.

SAY Point to the picture.
Look at the picture.
Point to the sentence that matches the picture.

3

A The dog is sleeping.

B The dog are barking.

C The dog is barking.

SAY Point to the picture.
Look at the picture.
Point to the sentence that matches the picture.

26

Guided Activity #4

1

A He are flying a kite in the sky.

B He is flying a kite in the sky.

C He is flying a bird in the sky.

2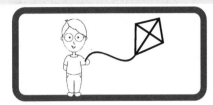

A The elephants is eating leafs.

B The elephant leaves.

C The elephant is eating leaves.

3

A The birds nests are eggs.

B There are eggs in the bird's nest.

C There eggs are in the birds nest.

Guided Activity #4

1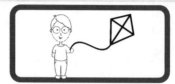

A He are flying a kite in the sky.

B He is flying a kite in the sky.

C He is flying a bird in the sky.

SAY Point to the picture.
Look at the picture.
Point to the sentence that matches the picture.

2

A The elephants is eating leafs.

B The elephant leaves.

C The elephant is eating leaves.

SAY Point to the picture.
Look at the picture.
Point to the sentence that matches the picture.

3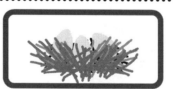

A The birds nests are eggs.

B There are eggs in the bird's nest.

C There eggs are in the birds nest.

SAY Point to the picture.
Look at the picture.
Point to the sentence that matches the picture.

28

Guided Activity #5

1

A She excited for her birthday?

B She is excited for her birthday!

C She are excited for her birthday.

2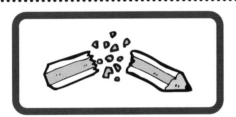

A The pencil is broked.

B The pencils are broke.

C The pencil broke in half.

3

A It raining outside.

B It is raining outside.

C It is rains outside.

29

Guided Activity #5

1

A She excited for her birthday?

B She is excited for her birthday!

C She are excited for her birthday.

 Point to the picture.
Look at the picture.
Point to the sentence that matches the picture.

2

A The pencil is broked.

B The pencils are broke.

C The pencil broke in half.

 Point to the picture.
Look at the picture.
Point to the sentence that matches the picture.

3

A It raining outside.

B It is raining outside.

C It is rains outside.

 Point to the picture.
Look at the picture.
Point to the sentence that matches the picture.

Reading: *Read and Choose a Sentence*

ELD Standards Record Sheet

<u>Directions:</u>
1. Look at the CA ELD standards (**BELOW**) that correspond to this section.
2. Reference these specific standards for the template Record Sheet.
3. Use the following template Record Sheet to monitor students' proficiency levels for the **GUIDED ACTIVITIES** in this section.
4. Fill out all the information. Circle, check, highlight the proficiency level. (*There is space for 20 students. Make additional copies, as needed*)
5. Retain for your records to be used during grading, parent/student conferences, lesson planning, ELD documentation, etc.

 Suggestion: You can make one copy of each guided activity and/or the student practice sheets and laminate them. Organize the laminated sheets onto a book ring. Now it'll be easily accessible for whole group, small group, one-on-one, centers, etc. Copy as many of the ELD Standards Record Sheet as you need and keep it handy along with the activities.

CA ELD Standards & Proficiency Levels
Part I: <u>Interacting in Meaningful Ways</u>
B.6 Reading/viewing closely

EMERGING (EM)	EXPANDING (EX)	BRIDGING (BR)
*Requires **Substantial** Support*	*Requires **Moderate** Support*	*Requires **Light** Support*

• Describes:
  ◦ Ideas
  ◦ phenomena (e.g., plant life cycle)
  ◦ text elements (e.g. main idea,
• characters, events)
• Reads and comprehends a select set of grade-level texts and multimedia with:
  ◦ Simple sentences
  ◦ Familiar vocabulary
  ◦ Support by graphics or pictures
• Requires substantial support
	• Describes in <u>greater details</u>:
	  ◦ Ideas
	  ◦ phenomena (e.g., how earthworms eat)
	  ◦ text elements (e.g. setting, events)
	• Reads and comprehends a <u>variety of</u> grade-level texts and multimedia with:
	  ◦ <u>Reliance on content and prior knowledge to obtain meaning from print</u>
	  ◦ Support by graphics or pictures
	• Requires <u>moderate</u> support
		• Describes <u>using key details</u>:
		  ◦ Ideas
		  ◦ phenomena (e.g., erosion)
		  ◦ text elements (e.g. central message, character traits)
		• Reads and comprehends a variety of grade-level texts and multimedia with:
		  ◦ <u>Limited comprehension difficulty</u>
		  ◦ <u>Comprehension of concrete and abstract topics</u>
		  ◦ <u>Recognize language subtleties</u>
		  ◦ Support by graphics or pictures
		• Requires <u>light</u> support

31

Reading: *Read and Choose a Sentence*

ELD Standards Record Sheet

Teacher: _____ **Class:** _____

Standards: *PI.B.6*　　　　　　**Guided Activities and Proficiency Levels:**

Students:	#1	#2	#3	#4	#5
	EM / EX / BR	EM / EX / BR	EM / EX / BR	EM / EX / BR	EM / EX / BR
	EM / EX / BR	EM / EX / BR	EM / EX / BR	EM / EX / BR	EM / EX / BR
	EM / EX / BR	EM / EX / BR	EM / EX / BR	EM / EX / BR	EM / EX / BR
	EM / EX / BR	EM / EX / BR	EM / EX / BR	EM / EX / BR	EM / EX / BR
	EM / EX / BR	EM / EX / BR	EM / EX / BR	EM / EX / BR	EM / EX / BR
	EM / EX / BR	EM / EX / BR	EM / EX / BR	EM / EX / BR	EM / EX / BR
	EM / EX / BR	EM / EX / BR	EM / EX / BR	EM / EX / BR	EM / EX / BR
	EM / EX / BR	EM / EX / BR	EM / EX / BR	EM / EX / BR	EM / EX / BR
	EM / EX / BR	EM / EX / BR	EM / EX / BR	EM / EX / BR	EM / EX / BR
	EM / EX / BR	EM / EX / BR	EM / EX / BR	EM / EX / BR	EM / EX / BR
	EM / EX / BR	EM / EX / BR	EM / EX / BR	EM / EX / BR	EM / EX / BR
	EM / EX / BR	EM / EX / BR	EM / EX / BR	EM / EX / BR	EM / EX / BR
	EM / EX / BR	EM / EX / BR	EM / EX / BR	EM / EX / BR	EM / EX / BR
	EM / EX / BR	EM / EX / BR	EM / EX / BR	EM / EX / BR	EM / EX / BR
	EM / EX / BR	EM / EX / BR	EM / EX / BR	EM / EX / BR	EM / EX / BR
	EM / EX / BR	EM / EX / BR	EM / EX / BR	EM / EX / BR	EM / EX / BR
	EM / EX / BR	EM / EX / BR	EM / EX / BR	EM / EX / BR	EM / EX / BR
	EM / EX / BR	EM / EX / BR	EM / EX / BR	EM / EX / BR	EM / EX / BR
	EM / EX / BR	EM / EX / BR	EM / EX / BR	EM / EX / BR	EM / EX / BR
	EM / EX / BR	EM / EX / BR	EM / EX / BR	EM / EX / BR	EM / EX / BR

Practice Activity #1

Name: ....

Directions: Draw a line to match the picture to the sentence.

example: 🚗 .... That is a car.

A	The man is at work.
B	The man are at work.
C	The men is at work.

Directions: Write one more sentence for the picture.

....

....

Directions: Draw a line to match the picture to the sentence.

example: 🚗 .... That is a car.

A	The boy are waiting for the school bus.
B	The boy is waiting for the school bus.
C	The boys are waiting for the bus.

Directions: Write one more sentence for the picture.

....

....

Practice Activity #2

Name: ....

Directions: Draw a line to match the picture to the sentence.

example: [car] .... That is a car.

A	The pig lives on the farm.
B	The pigs lifes on the farm.
C	The pig lives the farm.

Directions: Write one more sentence for the picture.

_____

_____

Directions: Draw a line to match the picture to the sentence.

example: [car] .... That is a car.

A	It is raining indoors.
B	It are rain outside.
C	It is raining outside.

Directions: Write one more sentence for the picture.

_____

_____

Practice Activity #3

Name: ....

Directions: Draw a line to match the picture to the sentence.

example: [car] .... That is a car.

A	The bird flying in the air.
B	The bird is flying through the air.
C	The birds are fly through the air.

Directions: Write one more sentence for the picture.

....

_____

....

_____

Directions: Draw a line to match the picture to the sentence.

example: [car] .... That is a car.

A	The house is on fire.
B	The home are on fire.
C	The house on fire.

Directions: Write one more sentence for the picture.

....

_____

....

Practice Activity #4

Name: ....

Directions: Draw a line to match the picture to the sentence.

example: [car] .... That is a car.

A | The man are fishing on the dock.

B | The men are fishing on the dock.

C | The man is fishing on the dock.

Directions: Write one more sentence for the picture.

....

....

Directions: Draw a line to match the picture to the sentence.

example: [car] .... That is a car.

A | The polar bear are looking.

B | The polar bear are hunt.

C | The polar bear is hunting.

Directions: Write one more sentence for the picture.

....

....

Practice Activity #5

Name: ....

Directions: Draw a line to match the picture to the sentence.

example: .... That is a car.

A	The turtle is swimming.
B	The turtle are swim.
C	The turtles is swimming.

Directions: Write one more sentence for the picture.

....

_____

_____

....

Directions: Draw a line to match the picture to the sentence.

example: .... That is a car.

A	The chefs is bakes.
B	The chef are bakes.
C	The chef is baking.

Directions: Write one more sentence for the picture.

....

_____

_____

....

Reading
Read a Short Informational Passage

This section includes:
- Guided Activities
- Teacher's ELD Standards Record Sheet
- Student Practice Activity:
  - Short Informational Passage Practice Activities

Alignment to CA ELD Standards:

Alignment to CCSS:

Part I: Interacting in Meaningful Ways

<u>B.6 Reading/viewing closely</u>
Reading closely literary and informational texts and viewing multimedia to determine how meaning is conveyed explicitly and implicitly through language

RL.2.1–7, 9–10; RI.2.1–7, 9–10; SL.2.2–3; L.2.3, 4, 6

Guided Activities Direction:

1. Show students the short informational passage and pictures.
2. Follow the teacher directions to have the students read the passages.
3. **Say** the **Teacher Script** (indicated by (**SAY**))
4. Guide students through:
   - Independently reading the short informational text
   - Comprehending the short informational text
   - Associating the pictures with the text
   - Answering basic comprehension questions
5. Review the questions and answers with the students. (questions are indicated by | **1** |)
6. Then have students practice with additional sheets.

Guided Activity #1

 SAY Show students the passage and questions.

Now you are going to read a short informational passage on your own and then answer the questions about the story.

Hummingbirds are among some of the smallest birds. They are best known for their ability to flap their wings extremely fast which creates a humming sound. They are also the only birds that can fly backwards.

Hummingbirds are small. They grow to be about 3-5 inches big. They have long, slender bills that allow them to drink the nectar from flowers. Long tongues are used to get to the sweet nectar inside the flowers. Unlike butterflies, hummingbirds do not land on a flower to drink the nectar. Instead, they hover by the flower as they flap their wings extremely fast. The wings move at such fast speeds that it seems like a blur.

Hummingbirds spend most of their time resting while perched on a tree somewhere. It takes a lot of energy to fly so fast, so they eat small meals throughout the day.

1 **Which image shows how a hummingbird eats?**

A   B   C

2 **Why are they called hummingbirds?**

    A. because they hum when they sing

    B. because of the sound their wings make

    C. because of the way they perch on a tree

3 **How do hummingbirds spend most of their time?**

    A. They feed on the nectar from the flowers.

    B. They look for other hummingbirds.

    C. They rest by perching on trees.

Guided Activity #1

Hummingbirds are among some of the smallest birds. They are best known for their ability to flap their wings extremely fast which creates a humming sound. They are also the only birds that can fly backwards.

Hummingbirds are small. They grow to be about 3-5 inches big. They have long, slender bills that allow them to drink the nectar from flowers. Long tongues are used to get to the sweet nectar inside the flowers. Unlike butterflies, hummingbirds do not land on a flower to drink the nectar. Instead, they hover by the flower as they flap their wings extremely fast. The wings move at such fast speeds that it seems like a blur.

Hummingbirds spend most of their time resting while perched on a tree somewhere. It takes a lot of energy to fly so fast, so they eat small meals throughout the day.

Guided Activity #1

Directions: Now answer the following questions about the short informational passage. Use the text and pictures to help you.

1 **Which image shows how a hummingbird eats?**

 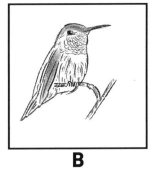 

| A | B | C |

2 **Why are they called hummingbirds?**

A. because they hum when they sing

B. because of the sound their wings make

C. because of the way they perch on a tree

3 **How do hummingbirds spend most of their time?**

A. They feed on the nectar from the flowers.

B. They look for other hummingbirds.

C. They rest by perching on trees.

Guided Activity #2

 SAY Show students the passage and questions.

Now you are going to read a short informational passage on your own and then answer the questions about the story.

Tides in the ocean are the periodic rising and falling of the ocean's water level. Tides are caused by the sun's and moon's gravitational pull on the Earth. Tides are also affected by the Earth's rotation on its axis. There are usually two tides in a day: high tide and low tide. These two events are usually 12 hours apart. Predicting the tides helps with sea navigation and other water activities.

High tide occurs when the water level is high. For instance, when it is high tide at the beach, the waves are higher and travel further onto the beach. Rocks and coral on the beach floor are covered by the water. High tide can cause large waves to crash onto the beach. This makes it dangerous to swim during these conditions.

Low tide occurs when the water level is low. The same rocks and coral that were covered by water during high tide are now exposed. This creates little tide pools where fish and other sea animals swim. People enjoy exploring these tide pools during the low tide.

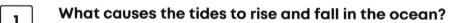

1 **What causes the tides to rise and fall in the ocean?**

  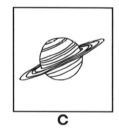

A   B   C

2 **What occurs during low tide?**

   A. The water level is low and exposes tide pools.

   B. The water level is high and makes it dangerous to swim.

   C. The water level does not change much.

3 **How often does high tide and low tide occur in a day?**

   A. High and low tides occur once a month.

   B. High and low tides occur every 30 days.

   C. High and low tides occur every 12 hours.

Guided Activity #2

 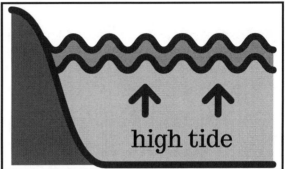

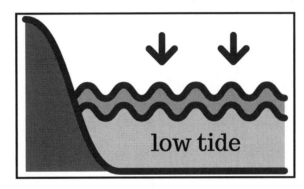

Tides in the ocean are the periodic rising and falling of the ocean's water level. Tides are caused by the sun's and moon's gravitational pull on the Earth. Tides are also affected by the Earth's rotation on its axis. There are usually two tides in a day: high tide and low tide. These two events are usually 12 hours apart. Predicting the tides helps with sea navigation and other water activities.

High tide occurs when the water level is high. For instance, when it is high tide at the beach, the waves are higher and travel further onto the beach. Rocks and coral on the beach floor are covered by the water. High tide can cause large waves to crash onto the beach. This makes it dangerous to swim during these conditions.

Low tide occurs when the water level is low. The same rocks and coral that were covered by water during high tide are now exposed. This creates little tide pools where fish and other sea animals swim. People enjoy exploring these tide pools during the low tide.

Guided Activity #2

Directions: Now answer the following questions about the short informational passage. Use the text and pictures to help you.

1 ## What causes the tides to rise and fall in the ocean?

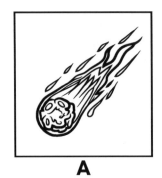  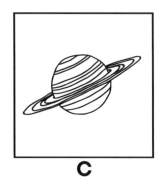

A   **B**   **C**

2 ## What occurs during low tide?

A. The water level is low and exposes tide pools.

B. The water level is high and makes it dangerous to swim.

C. The water level does not change much.

3 ## How often does high tide and low tide occur in a day?

A. High and low tides occur once a month.

B. High and low tides occur every 30 days.

C. High and low tides occur every 12 hours.

44

Guided Activity #3

 SAY Show students the passage and questions.

Now you are going to read a short informational passage on your own and then answer the questions about the story.

Squirrels are the cute, little bushy tailed rodents that people see scrambling up the neighborhood trees. These small mammals live everywhere except for Australia and Antarctica. There are over 280 different types of squirrels. They most commonly live in the trees or in holes in the ground.

Squirrels have long, slender bodies with soft fur. They have bushy tails and large eyes. Squirrels have excellent vision because of their large eyes. They mainly eat fruits, nuts, and seeds. However, they occasionally may eat small insects and tree bark as well. They have four large front teeth to help them gnaw on their food.

Squirrels are usually associated with their quick movements and habit of storing nuts and acorns. They can quickly run up a tree and jump great distances. Some people see squirrels as pest because these small rodents can destroy plants and crops. Squirrels can also carry diseases and, therefore, it is wise to leave these cute, furry animals alone.

1 **What do squirrels usually eat?**

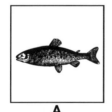  

A   B

2 **Squirrels live everywhere EXCEPT for what places?**

A. Australia and Antarctica

B. Antarctica and North America

C. Australia and Asia

3 **Why do some people consider squirrels to be pests?**

A. Squirrels are too quick and climb trees.

B. Squirrels eat and destroy plants and crops.

C. Squirrels have bushy tails and store acorns.

45

Guided Activity #3

Squirrels are the cute, little bushy tailed rodents that people see scrambling up the neighborhood trees. These small mammals live everywhere except for Australia and Antarctica. There are over 280 different types of squirrels. They most commonly live in the trees or in holes in the ground.

Squirrels have long, slender bodies with soft fur. They have bushy tails and large eyes. Squirrels have excellent vision because of their large eyes. They mainly eat fruits, nuts, and seeds. However, they occasionally may eat small insects and tree bark as well. They have four large front teeth to help them gnaw on their food.

Squirrels are usually associated with their quick movements and habit of storing nuts and acorns. They can quickly run up a tree and jump great distances. Some people see squirrels as pest because these small rodents can destroy plants and crops. Squirrels can also carry diseases and, therefore, it is wise to leave these cute, furry animals alone.

Guided Activity #3

Directions: Now answer the following questions about the short informational passage. Use the text and pictures to help you.

1 **What do squirrels usually eat?**

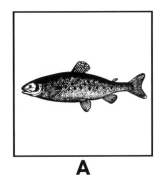
A

B

C

2 **Squirrels live everywhere EXCEPT for what places?**

A. Australia and Antarctica

B. Antarctica and North America

C. Australia and Asia

3 **Why do some people consider squirrels to be pests?**

A. Squirrels are too quick and climb trees.

B. Squirrels eat and destroy plants and crops.

C. Squirrels have bushy tails and store acorns.

Guided Activity #4

 SAY Show students the passage and questions.

Now you are going to read a short informational passage on your own and then answer the questions about the story.

You may know the President of the United States, but do you know exactly what the president's job is? The President of the United States is the head of the state and government. The president is also the Commander in Chief of the United States Armed Forces. The first President of the United States was George Washington.

As the head of the government's executive branch, the president's job is to enforce the laws passed by Congress. With the support of the Senate, the president has the power to make treaties and nominate justices to the Supreme Court. The president is elected by the American people.

A president can serve up to two terms. A term lasts four years so, therefore, a president can serve up to eight years. The main residence for the president is the White House located in Washington, D.C. The president travels on Air Force One which is a large airplane. Marine One is a helicopter that the president also uses. Secret service agents protect the president at all times. Their primary job is to keep the president safe from any threats.

1 **What does the president use to travel?**

A   B   C

2 **What is one of the president's primary jobs?**

A. To make sure that everyone votes

B. To enforce the laws passed by Congress

C. To write letters to the Senate

3 **How many years maximum can a president serve?**

A. 8 years

B. 4 years

C. 2 years

Guided Activity #4

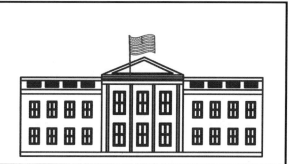

You may know the President of the United States, but do you know exactly what the president's job is? The President of the United States is the head of the state and government. The president is also the Commander in Chief of the United States Armed Forces. The first President of the United States was George Washington.

As the head of the government's executive branch, the president's job is to enforce the laws passed by Congress. With the support of the Senate, the president has the power to make treaties and nominate justices to the Supreme Court. The president is elected by the American people.

A president can serve up to two terms. A term lasts four years so, therefore, a president can serve up to eight years. The main residence for the president is the White House located in Washington, D.C. The president travels on Air Force One which is a large airplane. Marine One is a helicopter that the president also uses. Secret service agents protect the president at all times. Their primary job is to keep the president safe from any threats.

Guided Activity #4

Directions: Now answer the following questions about the short informational passage. Use the text and pictures to help you.

1 **What does the president use to travel?**

 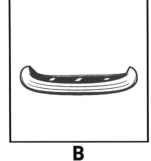 

A | B | C

2 **What is one of the president's primary jobs?**

A. To make sure that everyone votes

B. To enforce the laws passed by Congress

C. To write letters to the Senate

3 **How many years maximum can a president serve?**

A. 8 years

B. 4 years

C. 2 years

Guided Activity #5

 SAY Show students the passage and questions.
Now you are going to read a short informational passage on your own and then answer the questions about the story.

Beavers are mammals and are part of the rodent family that include mice and squirrels. Beavers are best known for their talented building skills of dams. Beavers live in rivers, lake, and streams in North America, Europe, and Asia.

Beavers are about 4 feet long with a flat, paddle-like tail. Their bodies are covered in thick, brown fur. They use their front feet to carry objects, while their webbed back feet help them to swim. Using their powerful jaws and teeth, beavers tear down small trees and bark to build their homes. Dams are the structures that beavers build using sticks, stones, and mud. The dam blocks the flow of water and creates a still pond where beavers like to live.

These furry and skillful animals eat mainly trees, twigs, and bark. They are mostly active at night. Working as a team or in pairs, beavers build the dams so that they can build their homes called lodges. The dams protect the beavers from predators and helps them find food during the winter months.

1 **What do beavers primarily eat?**

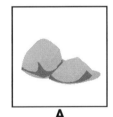 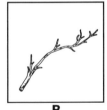 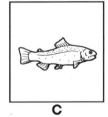

     A   **B**   **C**

2 **Why do beavers build dams?**

    A. to protect themselves from predators

    B. to create a private pool for themselves

    C. to catch fish in the rivers and streams

3 **What do beavers use to build the dams?**

    A. concrete, rocks, and mud

    B. sticks, stones, and mud

    C. just mud and sticks

Guided Activity #5

Beavers are mammals and are part of the rodent family that include mice and squirrels. Beavers are best known for their talented building skills of dams. Beavers live in rivers, lake, and streams in North America, Europe, and Asia.

Beavers are about 4 feet long with a flat, paddle-like tail. Their bodies are covered in thick, brown fur. They use their front feet to carry objects, while their webbed back feet help them to swim. Using their powerful jaws and teeth, beavers tear down small trees and bark to build their homes. Dams are the structures that beavers build using sticks, stones, and mud. The dam blocks the flow of water and creates a still pond where beavers like to live.

These furry and skillful animals eat mainly trees, twigs, and bark. They are mostly active at night. Working as a team or in pairs, beavers build the dams so that they can build their homes called lodges. The dams protect the beavers from predators and helps them find food during the winter months.

Guided Activity #5

Directions: Now answer the following questions about the short informational passage. Use the text and pictures to help you.

. . . .

1 **What do beavers primarily eat?**

A

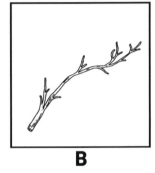
B

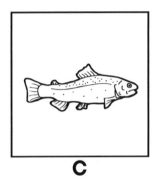
C

. . . .

2 **Why do beavers build dams?**

    A. to protect themselves from predators

    B. to create a private pool for themselves

    C. to catch fish in the rivers and streams

. . . .

3 **What do beavers use to build the dams?**

    A. concrete, rocks, and mud

    B. sticks, stones, and mud

    C. just mud and sticks

ELD Standards Record Sheet

Directions:

1. Look at the CA ELD standards (**BELOW**) that correspond to this section.
2. Reference these specific standards for the template Record Sheet.
3. Use the following template Record Sheet to monitor students' proficiency levels for the **GUIDED ACTIVITIES** in this section.
4. Fill out all the information. Circle, check, highlight the proficiency level. (*There is space for 20 students. Make additional copies, as needed*)
5. Retain for your records to be used during grading, parent/student conferences, lesson planning, ELD documentation, etc.

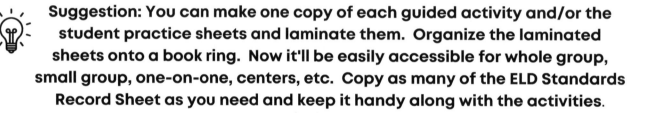

Suggestion: You can make one copy of each guided activity and/or the student practice sheets and laminate them. Organize the laminated sheets onto a book ring. Now it'll be easily accessible for whole group, small group, one-on-one, centers, etc. Copy as many of the ELD Standards Record Sheet as you need and keep it handy along with the activities.

CA ELD Standards & Proficiency Levels
Part I: Interacting in Meaningful Ways
B.6 Reading/viewing closely

EMERGING (EM)	EXPANDING (EX)	BRIDGING (BR)
*Requires **Substantial** Support*	*Requires **Moderate** Support*	*Requires **Light** Support*
<ul><li>*Describes:*<ul><li>*Ideas*</li><li>*phenomena (e.g., plant life cycle)*</li><li>*text elements (e.g. main idea,*</li></ul></li><li>*characters, events)*</li><li>*Reads and comprehends a select set of grade-level texts and multimedia with:*<ul><li>*Simple sentences*</li><li>*Familiar vocabulary*</li><li>*Support by graphics or pictures*</li></ul></li><li>*Requires substantial support*</li></ul>	<ul><li>*Describes in <u>greater details</u>:*<ul><li>*Ideas*</li><li>*phenomena (e.g., how earthworms eat)*</li><li>*text elements (e.g. setting, events)*</li></ul></li><li>*Reads and comprehends a <u>variety of</u> grade-level texts and multimedia with:*<ul><li>*<u>Reliance on content and prior knowledge to obtain meaning from print</u>*<ul><li>*Support by graphics or pictures*</li></ul></li></ul></li><li>*Requires <u>moderate</u> support*</li></ul>	<ul><li>*Describes <u>using key details</u>:*<ul><li>*Ideas*</li><li>*phenomena (e.g., erosion)*</li><li>*text elements (e.g. central message, character traits)*</li></ul></li><li>*Reads and comprehends a variety of grade-level texts and multimedia with:*<ul><li>*<u>Limited comprehension difficulty</u>*</li><li>*<u>Comprehension of concrete and abstract topics</u>*</li><li>*<u>Recognize language subtleties</u>*</li><li>*Support by graphics or pictures*</li></ul></li><li>*Requires <u>light</u> support*</li></ul>

54

Reading: *Read a Short Informational Passage*

ELD Standards Record Sheet

Teacher: _____ **Class:** _____

Standards: *PI.B.6*

Guided Activities and Proficiency Levels:

Students:	#1	#2	#3	#4	#5
	EM / EX / BR	EM / EX / BR	EM / EX / BR	EM / EX / BR	EM / EX / BR
	EM / EX / BR	EM / EX / BR	EM / EX / BR	EM / EX / BR	EM / EX / BR
	EM / EX / BR	EM / EX / BR	EM / EX / BR	EM / EX / BR	EM / EX / BR
	EM / EX / BR	EM / EX / BR	EM / EX / BR	EM / EX / BR	EM / EX / BR
	EM / EX / BR	EM / EX / BR	EM / EX / BR	EM / EX / BR	EM / EX / BR
	EM / EX / BR	EM / EX / BR	EM / EX / BR	EM / EX / BR	EM / EX / BR
	EM / EX / BR	EM / EX / BR	EM / EX / BR	EM / EX / BR	EM / EX / BR
	EM / EX / BR	EM / EX / BR	EM / EX / BR	EM / EX / BR	EM / EX / BR
	EM / EX / BR	EM / EX / BR	EM / EX / BR	EM / EX / BR	EM / EX / BR
	EM / EX / BR	EM / EX / BR	EM / EX / BR	EM / EX / BR	EM / EX / BR
	EM / EX / BR	EM / EX / BR	EM / EX / BR	EM / EX / BR	EM / EX / BR
	EM / EX / BR	EM / EX / BR	EM / EX / BR	EM / EX / BR	EM / EX / BR
	EM / EX / BR	EM / EX / BR	EM / EX / BR	EM / EX / BR	EM / EX / BR
	EM / EX / BR	EM / EX / BR	EM / EX / BR	EM / EX / BR	EM / EX / BR
	EM / EX / BR	EM / EX / BR	EM / EX / BR	EM / EX / BR	EM / EX / BR
	EM / EX / BR	EM / EX / BR	EM / EX / BR	EM / EX / BR	EM / EX / BR
	EM / EX / BR	EM / EX / BR	EM / EX / BR	EM / EX / BR	EM / EX / BR
	EM / EX / BR	EM / EX / BR	EM / EX / BR	EM / EX / BR	EM / EX / BR
	EM / EX / BR	EM / EX / BR	EM / EX / BR	EM / EX / BR	EM / EX / BR
	EM / EX / BR	EM / EX / BR	EM / EX / BR	EM / EX / BR	EM / EX / BR

Practice Activity #1

Name: ....

Directions: Practice reading the short passage aloud:

☐ To myself   ☐ With a partner   ☐ With an adult

When you look up in the sky you see big, puffy clouds. However, sometimes the clouds are dark and gray. Those clouds are storm clouds. Rain comes from storm clouds. It is the precipitation part of the water cycle.

During a storm, rain falls from the clouds. It can be a light drizzle or heavy rainfall. When too much rain falls in a place in a short period of time, flooding can occur. Flooding can cause a lot of damage, such as mudslides and flooding of peoples' homes.

Rain is vital, or important, for many reasons. We need the rain to water the trees and plants. The trees and plants need the rain to live and grow. We also need the rain for our daily use, such as bathing or cooking or watering the crops. Rain also cools down the Earth's temperature. It prevents areas from experiencing droughts, which is when there is a long period of time with no water. Therefore, it is important to have an annual, or yearly, rainfall.

However, sometimes rain can be fun. Puddles form on the ground and are fun to jump and splash in! Some people collect rain water to water their plants and gardens. Rain is a vital part of the water cycle and helps all living things on the planet.

Directions: Write a short summary of what you just read.

Practice Activity #1

Name: ....

Directions: Complete the graphic organizer about the short passage. Use the information in the text to help you. Then answer the following questions.

Main Idea
What is the passage mostly about?

Fact #1	Fact #2	Fact #3

1 What happens when too much rain falls in a short period of time?

A the rivers and streams flow faster into the ocean

B quickly rising waters can cause floods

C too much water can water plants and trees

2 How is rainfall beneficial for the Earth?

A rainfall doesn't help the planet

B rainfall helps to moderate the ocean levels by keeping it low

C rainfall regulates the Earth's temperature and keeps the planet cool

Practice Activity #2

Name: ....

Directions: Practice reading the short passage aloud:

☐ To myself   ☐ With a partner   ☐ With an adult

Have you ever looked closely at a bee? Bees are insects and are important to our environment. They can be found buzzing around the flowers and plants. Some people see them as a nuisance, however these buzzing insects are crucial to the pollination of plants and crops.

Bees are yellow with black stripes. They have tiny little hairs all over their bodies. Their bodies have three main parts: head, thorax, and abdomen. Two antennas on their heads help them feel and smell. Their wings help them to fly.

Bees are attracted to blooming flowers. They like the nectar in the flowers. The nectar is sweet and the bees use it for energy. Bees are very intelligent and have excellent memories. They can always find their way back to their hives. Bees also take the pollen from flower to flower. This helps the flowers to spread their seeds and grow. Some bees use the pollen from the flowers for energy.

Bees also have stingers that can sting people. Some people are allergic to a bee sting. It's best to just observe them from afar! However, not all bees sting. Bees live in large groups called colonies. The bees have different jobs in the colonies. There are worker bees and a queen bee. These fascinating insects are more than just honey producers!

Directions: Write a short summary of what you just read.

Practice Activity #2

Name: ···

Directions: Complete the graphic organizer about the short passage. Use the information in the text to help you. Then answer the following questions.

Main Idea
What is the passage mostly about?

Fact #1	Fact #2	Fact #3

1 Why are bees vital to the environment?

   A They help with the pollination of plants and flowers.

   B They help with the honey supply for humans.

   C They help people learn about the dangers of nature.

2 What do bees look like?

   A black with yellow stripes

   B yellow with white stripes

   C yellow with black stripes

Practice Activity #3

Name: ....

Directions: Practice reading the short passage aloud:

☐ To myself   ☐ With a partner   ☐ With an adult

Earth has many biomes, or large areas with similar plants, climate, and animal habitats. One type of biome is a rainforest. A rainforest has a diverse number of plants and animals. The climate is usually cool, humid and a rainforest receives a considerable amount of rainfall.

Tall, towering trees reach high up into the sky in a rainforest. There are many trees in the rainforest and they form a canopy over the forest floor. The canopy is similar to an umbrella. The canopy of trees keeps the rainforest's temperatures near the ground cool and moist. It is very lush and green in this environment. Scientists are still discovering new species of plants all the time.

Many animals call the rainforest home. Snakes, spiders, exotic birds, and monkeys thrive in this habitat. Animals and insects can find plenty of food and water. The thick plants and trees offer great places to hide.

It is called a rainforest because it receives a lot of rain. Some rainforest can get as much as 10 feet of rain in a year! The temperature is always cool and humid. Rainforests are one of the most diverse biomes in the world!

Directions: Write a short summary of what you just read.

....

....

....

....

Practice Activity #3

Name: ....

Directions: Complete the graphic organizer about the short passage. Use the information in the text to help you. Then answer the following questions.

Main Idea
What is the passage mostly about?

Fact #1	Fact #2	Fact #3

1 Why is the rainforest biome so lush and green?

   A it receives little to no rain, but the plants and trees still grow

   B it has plants that stay green all year round

   C it receives plenty of rainfall every year for the plants and trees to grow

2 What is the climate like in a rainforest?

   A it is humid and cool

   B it is hot and dry

   C it is humid and dry

Practice Activity #4

Name: ....

Directions: Practice reading the short passage aloud:

☐ To myself   ☐ With a partner   ☐ With an adult

Have you ever been on an airplane or rode in a car? People can travel and move around in many ways. This is called transportation. There are many modes of transportation, whether it is by land, sea, or air. Transportation has changed a lot through the years. People can not travel around the world in a shorter amount of time.

One very common mode of transportation is by car. A car is frequently used to get from one place to another. People use cars to travel daily. Cars have become more efficient and advanced. There are even electric cars now.

Another way to travel is by airplane. Airplanes fly through the air. They can transport a lot of passengers and things. Airplanes allow us to travel to different places in the world quicker. People can travel across the oceans without having to ride aboard a ship. People can also travel by train. Trains can also transport a lot of supplies and materials across the land.

When traveling by sea, people get aboard big boats and ships. Cruise ships are floating hotels that take travelers to different places. Cargo ships transport supplies and materials all over the world. These cargo ships are a vital part of the world's supply chain. Transportation has changed how we navigate the world!

Directions: Write a short summary of what you just read.

_____

....

_____

....

_____

....

_____

Practice Activity #4

Name: ....

Directions: Complete the graphic organizer about the short passage. Use the information in the text to help you. Then answer the following questions.

Main Idea
What is the passage mostly about?

Fact #1

Fact #2

Fact #3

---

1 How have airplanes changed the way we travel?

   A people can learn how to fly higher

   B people can travel faster and further around the world

   C people can feel what it's like to be a bird

2 Why are ships important to the world's supply chain?

   A ships helps people navigate the oceans

   B cruise ships carry people to different vacation destinations

   C cargo ships transport supplies and materials around the world

Practice Activity #5

Name: ....

Directions: Practice reading the short passage aloud:

☐ To myself   ☐ With a partner   ☐ With an adult

Do you have a pet? Is it a dog or cat? Or maybe it's something completely unusual. Many people have pets. Pets provide people with plenty of love and happiness. Some studies have shown that people with pets are happier and tend to live longer. People can have many different kinds of pets.

The most common kind of pets are dogs and cats. Dogs are active and enjoy running around and playing. They have a lot of energy and require daily walking and exercise. Other people prefer to have cats. Cats, in general, are usually more calm. They keep to themselves and require less activity. However, cats need just as much love and attention as a dog.

Some people have fish as a pet. Fish can be kept in a fish tank or aquarium. They require very little maintenance, except for a clean tank and plenty of fish food. Some people have fresh water fish while others have saltwater fish tanks.

A few people keep exotic pets, such as parrots and reptiles. Lizards can be unusual pets, but are still pets nonetheless. Hamsters and turtles are other types of pets. Pets are part of the family and are really loved. They make great companions and friends. Having a pet is a big responsibility and should be taken seriously.

Directions: Write a short summary of what you just read.

_____

_____

_____

_____

Practice Activity #5

Name: ....

Directions: Complete the graphic organizer about the short passage. Use the information in the text to help you. Then answer the following questions.

Main Idea
What is the passage mostly about?

Fact #1	Fact #2	Fact #3

1 Why do some people have pets?

   A people have pets to go exercise at the park with

   B people have pets to keep their kids busy

   C pets provide people with love and happiness

2 What is the difference between having a dog vs. a cat as a pet?

   A dogs are more active while cats tend to keep to themselves

   B dogs eat more food than cats

   C dogs have just as much energy as cats

Reading
Read a Literary Passage

This section includes:
- Guided Activities
- Teacher's ELD Standards Record Sheet
- Student Practice Activities:
  - Literary passage practice activities

Alignment to CA ELD Standards:	Alignment to CCSS:
Part I: Interacting in Meaningful Ways	
<u>B.6 Reading/viewing closely</u>	
Reading closely literary and informational texts and viewing multimedia to determine how meaning is conveyed explicitly and implicitly through language	RL.2.1–7, 9–10; RI.2.1–7, 9–10; SL.2.2–3; L.2.3, 4, 6
Part I: Interacting in Meaningful Ways	
<u>B.7 Evaluating language choices</u>	
Evaluating how well writers and speakers use language to support ideas and opinions with details or reasons depending on modality, text type, purpose, audience, topic, and content area	RL.2.3–4, 6; RI.2.2, 6, 8; SL.2.3; L.2.3–6
Part I: Interacting in Meaningful Ways	
<u>B.8 Analyzing language choice</u>	
Analyzing how writers and speakers use vocabulary and other language resources for specific purposes (to explain, persuade, entertain, etc.) depending on modality, text type, purpose, audience, topic, and content area	RL.2.4–5; RI.2.4–5; SL.2.3; L.2.3–6

Reading
Read a Literary Passage

- -

Alignment to CA ELD Standards:

Part II: Learning About How English Works
A.1 Structuring Cohesive Texts
Understanding text structure

Part II: Learning About How English Works
A.2 Structuring Cohesive Texts
Understanding Cohesion

Alignment to CCSS:

RL.2.5; RI.2.5; W.2.1–5;
SL.2.4

RL.2.5; RI.2.5; W.2.1–4;
SL.2.4; L.2.1, 3

- -

Guided Activities Direction:

1. Show students the literary passage, pictures, and questions.
2. Follow the teacher directions.
3. **Say** the **Teacher Script** (indicated by (**SAY**))
4. Guide students through:
   - Reading the text independently
   - Comprehending the text
   - Associating the pictures with the text
   - Answering basic comprehension questions
5. Review the questions and answers with the students. (questions are indicated by | **1** |)
6. Then have students practice with additional sheets.

Reading: *Read a Literary Passage*

Guided Activity #1

 SAY Show students the passage and questions.
Now you are going to read a passage on your own and answer the questions about the passage.

It was a cool fall day. Jacob and his friend were out riding their bikes. They were riding through the neighborhood park when they heard a little whimper come from behind a tree.

"What was that?" Jacob said to his friend. "It sounded like something crying." Both boys stopped and got off their bikes. They stood still for a minute until they heard the whimpering sound again.

"It's coming from behind that tree," said Jacob's friend. They ran to look behind the tree where the sound was coming from. "It's a little puppy!" exclaimed both boys at the same time.

The little puppy was huddled behind the tree and whimpering. "I think it's lost," said Jacob. "We should see if we could find its owner." They checked the tag on the puppy's collar. It said Mrs. Robinson. "That's my neighbor!" exclaimed Jacob.

They carefully picked up the puppy and walked back home with their bikes. They returned the lost puppy to a very grateful Mrs. Robinson. She gave the boys fresh baked cookies as a thank you.

1 **Why did Jacob and his friend stop riding their bikes?**

    A. They were feeling tired.

    B. They heard a whimper.

    C. They were lost.

2 **What did the boys find behind the tree?**

    A   **B**   **C**

3 **What happened at the end of the story?**

    A. The boys went home.

    B. The boys returned their bikes.

    C. The boys returned the puppy.

Guided Activity #1

It was a cool fall day. Jacob and his friend were out riding their bikes. They were riding through the neighborhood park when they heard a little whimper come from behind a tree.

"What was that?" Jacob said to his friend. "It sounded like something crying." Both boys stopped and got off their bikes. They stood still for a minute until they heard the whimpering sound again.

"It's coming from behind that tree," said Jacob's friend. They ran to look behind the tree where the sound was coming from. "It's a little puppy!" exclaimed both boys at the same time.

The little puppy was huddled behind the tree and whimpering. "I think it's lost," said Jacob. "We should see if we could find its owner." They checked the tag on the puppy's collar. It said Mrs. Robinson. "That's my neighbor!" exclaimed Jacob.

They carefully picked up the puppy and walked back home with their bikes. They returned the lost puppy to a very grateful Mrs. Robinson. She gave the boys fresh baked cookies as a thank you.

Guided Activity #1

Now have the students read and answer the questions for the passage. Guide the students through answering the comprehension questions by using both the pictures and sentences of the story.

∙∙

1 **Why did Jacob and his friend stop riding their bikes?**

 A. They were feeling tired.

 B. They heard a whimper.

 C. They were lost.

∙∙

2 **What did the boys find behind the tree?**

 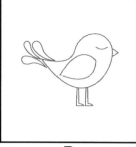 

  A   **B**   **C**

∙∙

3 **What happened at the end of the story?**

 A. The boys went home.

 B. The boys returned their bikes.

 C. The boys returned the puppy.

Reading: *Read a Literary Passage*

Guided Activity #2

SAY Show students the passage and questions.
Now you are going to read a passage on your own and answer the questions about the passage.

• •

It was the day of the big soccer game. Ken was excited to play with his team. They were close to winning the championship for their school. Before leaving, Ken searched for his soccer ball, but he couldn't find it.

"Oh no! Where is it?" exclaimed Ken. "I remember putting it back in the closet after I finished practicing yesterday." Feeling frustrated and worried that he was going to miss the big game, Ken started crying. He had lost his soccer ball.

"What's wrong, dear?" asked Ken's mother.

"I can't find my soccer ball!" Ken told her. "Don't worry, we'll find it somewhere here," she comforted Ken. His mother helped him look around the house for the ball.

After looking in his room and the kitchen, they still didn't see the ball. When they went to the dining room they found the ball under the table. Ken quickly retrieved it.

"Oh there it is! Thank you for your help, mom!" Ken said and then hugged his mom. He was relieved and happy. Now he was ready to win the big game!

• •

1 **How was Ken feeling when he couldn't find his ball?**

    A. He was feeling frustrated and worried.

    B. He was feeling excited and happy.

    C. He was feeling nervous and joyful.

• •

2 **Where did they find the soccer ball?**

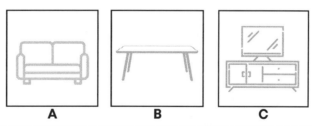

        A   B   C

• •

3 **How did Ken feel at the end of the story?**

    A. Ken felt angry and frustrated.

    B. Ken felt relieved and happy.

    C. Ken felt disappointed and sad.

Guided Activity #2

It was the day of the big soccer game. Ken was excited to play with his team. They were close to winning the championship for their school. Before leaving, Ken searched for his soccer ball, but he couldn't find it.

"Oh no! Where is it?" exclaimed Ken. "I remember putting it back in the closet after I finished practicing yesterday." Feeling frustrated and worried that he was going to miss the big game, Ken started crying. He had lost his soccer ball.

"What's wrong, dear?" asked Ken's mother.

"I can't find my soccer ball!" Ken told her. "Don't worry, we'll find it somewhere here," she comforted Ken. His mother helped him look around the house for the ball.

After looking in his room and the kitchen, they still didn't see the ball. When they went to the dining room they found the ball under the table. Ken quickly retrieved it.

"Oh there it is! Thank you for your help, mom!" Ken said and then hugged his mom. He was relieved and happy. Now he was ready to win the big game!

Guided Activity #2

Now have the students read and answer the questions for the passage. Guide the students through answering the comprehension questions by using both the pictures and sentences of the story.

· ·

1 **How was Ken feeling when he couldn't find his ball?**

    A. He was feeling frustrated and worried.

    B. He was feeling excited and happy.

    C. He was feeling nervous and joyful.

· ·

2 **Where did they find the soccer ball?**

 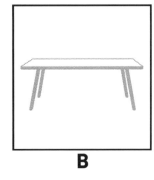 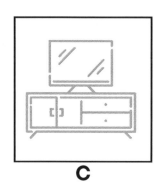

    A   **B**   **C**

· ·

3 **How did Ken feel at the end of the story?**

    A. Ken felt angry and frustrated.

    B. Ken felt relieved and happy.

    C. Ken felt disappointed and sad.

Reading: *Read a Literary Passage*

Guided Activity #3

 SAY Show students the passage and questions.
Now you are going to read a passage on your own and answer the questions about the passage.

Today was a big day at school. Maria was going to share out during show and tell in her 2nd grade class. She had been looking forward to her turn for a few days now. Her mother had helped her prepare for her presentation.

"Good luck today, honey," said her mother as she was dropping her off at school. "You'll do great!"

"Thanks mom, I hope the class likes my drawing!" replied Maria. She had painted a portrait of her family. She looked inside her backpack just to be sure it was there.

"Oh no! It's not in my backpack! Where could it be?" cried Maria. Maria and her mother glanced around the front seat of the car. They didn't see the painting. Maria started to feel sad.

Suddenly, her mother reached into the back seat of the car and picked up the painting. It had slipped onto the floor in the back. Maria felt happy and was ready to share out her family portrait.

1 **Why was it a big day at school for Maria?**

 A. It was her turn for show and tell.

 B. It was the day of the spelling bee.

 C. It was going to be painting time.

2 **What was Maria going to share with her class?**

 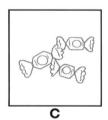

  A   **B**   **C**

3 **How did Maria's mom help her?**

 A. She presented to the class with Maria.

 B. She packed her a delicious lunch.

 C. She found the painting in the back seat.

Guided Activity #3

Today was a big day at school. Maria was going to share out during show and tell in her 2nd grade class. She had been looking forward to her turn for a few days now. Her mother had helped her prepare for her presentation.

"Good luck today, honey," said her mother as she was dropping her off at school. "You'll do great!"

"Thanks mom, I hope the class likes my drawing!" replied Maria. She had painted a portrait of her family. She looked inside her backpack just to be sure it was there.

"Oh no! It's not in my backpack! Where could it be?" cried Maria. Maria and her mother glanced around the front seat of the car. They didn't see the painting. Maria started to feel sad.

Suddenly, her mother reached into the back seat of the car and picked up the painting. It had slipped onto the floor in the back. Maria felt happy and was ready to share out her family portrait.

Guided Activity #3

Now have the students read and answer the questions for the passage. Guide the students through answering the comprehension questions by using both the pictures and sentences of the story.

• •

1 **Why was it a big day at school for Maria?**

> **A. It was her turn for show and tell.**
>
> **B. It was the day of the spelling bee.**
>
> **C. It was going to be painting time.**

• •

2 **What was Maria going to share with her class?**

 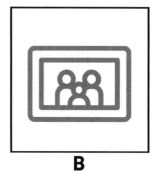 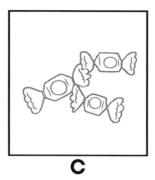

| A | B | C |

• •

3 **How did Maria's mom help her?**

> **A. She presented to the class with Maria.**
>
> **B. She packed her a delicious lunch.**
>
> **C. She found the painting in the back seat.**

Reading: *Read a Literary Passage*

Guided Activity #4

It was a relaxing Saturday afternoon. Our family usually enjoyed doing a fun activity together. My dad decided to take my brother and I to our favorite place. We went to the local public library.

"What a great idea, dad!" my brother and I both said together. The library was our favorite place because we enjoyed reading. We have read many of the books at the library, but there was so much more to read!

At the library, we all looked at the books on the neatly lined shelves. My brother and I chose our books and sat down on the rug to read. I read a book about space. My brother had a book about animals.

"I think I'll read this one," said my dad. He had chosen a book about dinosaurs. He had always been fascinated with fossils and prehistoric history.

We spent a few hours reading our books. It was a lovely Saturday afternoon at the library.

1 **Where did the family go?**

    A. to the store

    B. to the library

    C. to the park

2 **Where did the family sit?**

    A   **B**   **C**

3 **What book did the dad read?**

    A. a book about dinosaurs

    B. a book about trees

    C. a book about animals

Guided Activity #4

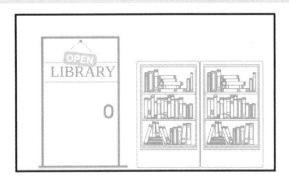 

It was a relaxing Saturday afternoon. Our family usually enjoyed doing a fun activity together. My dad decided to take my brother and I to our favorite place. We went to the local public library.

"What a great idea, dad!" my brother and I both said together. The library was our favorite place because we enjoyed reading. We have read many of the books at the library, but there was so much more to read!

At the library, we all looked at the books on the neatly lined shelves. My brother and I chose our books and sat down on the rug to read. I read a book about space. My brother had a book about animals.

"I think I'll read this one," said my dad. He had chosen a book about dinosaurs. He had always been fascinated with fossils and prehistoric history.

We spent a few hours reading our books. It was a lovely Saturday afternoon at the library.

Guided Activity #4

Now have the students read and answer the questions for the passage. Guide the students through answering the comprehension questions by using both the pictures and sentences of the story.

. . . .

1   **Where did the family go?**

     A. to the store

     B. to the library

     C. to the park

. . . .

2   **Where did the family sit?**

     A   **B**   **C**

. . . .

3   **What book did the dad read?**

     A. a book about dinosaurs

     B. a book about trees

     C. a book about animals

Reading: *Read a Literary Passage*

Guided Activity #5

SAY Show students the passage and questions.
Now you are going to read a passage on your own and answer the questions about the passage.

Ms. Kim was a second grade teacher. She loved teaching her class about science. Her students were always excited to learn something new during science time. Ms. Kim had a special surprise planned for her class during their lesson today.

"Alright class, today we have a special surprise!" Ms. Kim told her students. "We are going to learn about butterflies and I have something to share with all of you."

Her students were very excited and couldn't wait to see what surprise their teacher had for them. After a fun and interesting lesson about butterflies, Ms. Kim gathered her students to the carpet.

"Alright boys and girls, you did a wonderful job today with our science lesson. Here is our surprise!" said Ms. Kim as she uncovered a box that had a glass tank with a beautiful butterfly inside. "This is our class butterfly for the day! We are going to go outside and release it." The students all cheered with joy.

1 **Why was Ms. Kim excited about the science lesson today?**

    A. She was going to talk about space.

    B. She was going to show a video about butterflies.

    C. She had a surprise for the students.

2 **What was the science lesson about?**

    A   **B**   **C**

3 **What was Ms. Kim's surprise for the class?**

    A. She brought them stickers.

    B. She showed them a butterfly.

    C. She showed them a new book.

Guided Activity #5

Ms. Kim was a second grade teacher. She loved teaching her class about science. Her students were always excited to learn something new during science time. Ms. Kim had a special surprise planned for her class during their lesson today.

"Alright class, today we have a special surprise!" Ms. Kim told her students. "We are going to learn about butterflies and I have something to share with all of you."

Her students were very excited and couldn't wait to see what surprise their teacher had for them. After a fun and interesting lesson about butterflies, Ms. Kim gathered her students to the carpet.

"Alright boys and girls, you did a wonderful job today with our science lesson. Here is our surprise!" said Ms. Kim as she uncovered a box that had a glass tank with a beautiful butterfly inside. "This is our class butterfly for the day! We are going to go outside and release it." The students all cheered with joy.

Guided Activity #5

Now have the students read and answer the questions for the passage. Guide the students through answering the comprehension questions by using both the pictures and sentences of the story.

. . . .

1 **Why was Ms. Kim excited about the science lesson today?**

   A. She was going to talk about space.

   B. She was going to show a video about butterflies.

   C. She had a surprise for the students.

. . . .

2 **What was the science lesson about?**

   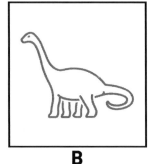   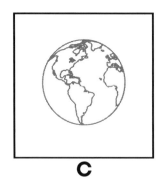

   A   **B**   **C**

. . . .

3 **What was Ms. Kim's surprise for the class?**

   A. She brought them stickers.

   B. She showed them a butterfly.

   C. She showed them a new book.

ELD Standards Record Sheet

<u>Directions:</u>

1. Look at the CA ELD standards (**BELOW**) that correspond to this section.
2. Reference these specific standards for the template Record Sheet.
3. Use the following template Record Sheet to monitor students' proficiency levels for the **GUIDED ACTIVITIES** in this section.
4. Fill out all the information. Circle, check, highlight the proficiency level. (*There is space for 20 students. Make additional copies, as needed*)
5. Retain for your records to be used during grading, parent/student conferences, lesson planning, ELD documentation, etc.

 Suggestion: You can make one copy of each guided activity and/or the student practice sheets and laminate them. Organize the laminated sheets onto a book ring. Now it'll be easily accessible for whole group, small group, one-on-one, centers, etc. Copy as many of the ELD Standards Record Sheet as you need and keep it handy along with the activities.

CA ELD Standards & Proficiency Levels
<u>**Part I:** Interacting in Meaningful Ways</u>
B.6 Reading/viewing closely

EMERGING (EM)	EXPANDING (EX)	BRIDGING (BR)
*Requires **Substantial** Support*	*Requires **Moderate** Support*	*Requires **Light** Support*

• Describes:
  ○ Ideas
  ○ phenomena (e.g., plant life cycle)
  ○ text elements (e.g. main idea,
• characters, events)
• Reads and comprehends a select set of grade-level texts and multimedia with:
  ○ Simple sentences
  ○ Familiar vocabulary
  ○ Support by graphics or pictures
• Requires substantial support
	• Describes in <u>greater details</u>:
	  ○ Ideas
	  ○ phenomena (e.g., how earthworms eat)
	  ○ text elements (e.g. setting, events)
	• Reads and comprehends a <u>variety of</u> grade-level texts and multimedia with:
	  ○ <u>Reliance on content and prior</u>
	• <u>knowledge to obtain meaning from print</u>
	  ○ Support by graphics or pictures
	• Requires <u>moderate</u> support
		• Describes <u>using key details</u>:
		  ○ Ideas
		  ○ phenomena (e.g., erosion)
		  ○ text elements (e.g. central message, character traits)
		• Reads and comprehends a variety of grade-level texts and multimedia with:
		  ○ <u>Limited comprehension difficulty</u>
		  ○ <u>Comprehension of concrete and abstract topics</u>
		  ○ <u>Recognize language subtleties</u>
		  ○ Support by graphics or pictures
		• Requires <u>light</u> support

ELD Standards Record Sheet

CA ELD Standards & Proficiency Levels
Part I: Interacting in Meaningful Ways
B.7 Evaluating Language Choices

EMERGING (EM)	EXPANDING (EX)	BRIDGING (BR)
Requires **Substantial** Support	Requires **Moderate** Support	Requires **Light** Support
• Describe the language writers or speakers use to present an idea:(e.g. the words and phrases used to describe a character) • Requires prompting and substantial support	• Describe the language writers or speakers use to present or <u>support</u> an idea: (e.g. the author's choice of vocabulary or phrasing to portray characters, places, or real people) • Requires prompting and <u>moderate</u> support	• Describe <u>how well writers or speakers use specific language resources to support an opinion</u> or present an idea: (e.g. whether the vocabulary used to present evidence is strong enough) • Requires prompting and <u>light</u> support

CA ELD Standards & Proficiency Levels
Part I: Interacting in Meaningful Ways
B.8 Analyzing Language Choices

EMERGING (EM)	EXPANDING (EX)	BRIDGING (BR)
Requires **Substantial** Support	Requires **Moderate** Support	Requires **Light** Support
• Distinguish how two different frequently used words: (e.g. describing a character as happy vs. angry) • Produce a different effect on the audience	• Distinguish how two different words <u>with similar meaning</u>: (e.g. describing a character as happy vs ecstatic) • Produce <u>shades of meaning</u> and a different effect on the audience	• Distinguish how <u>multiple</u> different words with similar meaning: (e.g. pleased vs happy vs ecstatic, heard vs knew vs believed) • Produce shades of meaning and a different effect on the audience

ELD Standards Record Sheet

CA ELD Standards & Proficiency Levels
Part II: Learning About How English Works
A.1 Understanding text structure

EMERGING (EM)	EXPANDING (EX)	BRIDGING (BR)
Requires **Substantial** Support	Requires **Moderate** Support	Requires **Light** Support
• Apply understanding of how text types are organized to express ideas (e.g. how a story is organized sequentially) • Comprehend & compose texts with substantial support • Comprehend & write texts in shared language activities (guided by teacher, peers, and sometimes independently)	• Apply understanding of how <u>different</u> text types are organized to express ideas (e.g. how a story is organized sequentially with predictable stages vs how an information report is organized by topic and details) • Comprehend & write texts (w/ <u>increasing independence</u>)	• Apply understanding of how different text types are organized <u>predictably</u> to express ideas (e.g. a narrative vs an informative/explanatory text vs an opinion text) • Comprehend & write texts (<u>independently</u>)

CA ELD Standards & Proficiency Levels
Part II: Learning About How English Works
A.2 Understanding cohesion

EMERGING (EM)	EXPANDING (EX)	BRIDGING (BR)
Requires **Substantial** Support	Requires **Moderate** Support	Requires **Light** Support
• Apply basic understanding of how ideas, events, or reasons are linked throughout a text • Uses more everyday connecting words or phrases (e.g. today, then) • Comprehend & write texts in shared language activities (guided by teacher, peers, and sometimes independently)	• Apply understanding of how ideas, events, or reasons are linked throughout a text • Uses a <u>growing number</u> of connecting words or phrases (e.g. after a long time, first/next) • Comprehend & write texts (w/ <u>increasing independence</u>)	• Apply understanding of how ideas, events, or reasons are linked throughout a text • Uses a <u>variety</u> of connecting words or phrases (e.g. for example, after that, suddenly) • Comprehend & write texts (<u>independently</u>)

Reading: *Read a Literary Passage*

ELD Standards Record Sheet

Teacher: _____ **Class:** _____

Standards: *PI.B.6*   **Guided Activities and Proficiency Levels:**

Students:	#1	#2	#3	#4	#5
	EM / EX / BR	EM / EX / BR	EM / EX / BR	EM / EX / BR	EM / EX / BR
	EM / EX / BR	EM / EX / BR	EM / EX / BR	EM / EX / BR	EM / EX / BR
	EM / EX / BR	EM / EX / BR	EM / EX / BR	EM / EX / BR	EM / EX / BR
	EM / EX / BR	EM / EX / BR	EM / EX / BR	EM / EX / BR	EM / EX / BR
	EM / EX / BR	EM / EX / BR	EM / EX / BR	EM / EX / BR	EM / EX / BR
	EM / EX / BR	EM / EX / BR	EM / EX / BR	EM / EX / BR	EM / EX / BR
	EM / EX / BR	EM / EX / BR	EM / EX / BR	EM / EX / BR	EM / EX / BR
	EM / EX / BR	EM / EX / BR	EM / EX / BR	EM / EX / BR	EM / EX / BR
	EM / EX / BR	EM / EX / BR	EM / EX / BR	EM / EX / BR	EM / EX / BR
	EM / EX / BR	EM / EX / BR	EM / EX / BR	EM / EX / BR	EM / EX / BR
	EM / EX / BR	EM / EX / BR	EM / EX / BR	EM / EX / BR	EM / EX / BR
	EM / EX / BR	EM / EX / BR	EM / EX / BR	EM / EX / BR	EM / EX / BR
	EM / EX / BR	EM / EX / BR	EM / EX / BR	EM / EX / BR	EM / EX / BR
	EM / EX / BR	EM / EX / BR	EM / EX / BR	EM / EX / BR	EM / EX / BR
	EM / EX / BR	EM / EX / BR	EM / EX / BR	EM / EX / BR	EM / EX / BR
	EM / EX / BR	EM / EX / BR	EM / EX / BR	EM / EX / BR	EM / EX / BR
	EM / EX / BR	EM / EX / BR	EM / EX / BR	EM / EX / BR	EM / EX / BR
	EM / EX / BR	EM / EX / BR	EM / EX / BR	EM / EX / BR	EM / EX / BR
	EM / EX / BR	EM / EX / BR	EM / EX / BR	EM / EX / BR	EM / EX / BR
	EM / EX / BR	EM / EX / BR	EM / EX / BR	EM / EX / BR	EM / EX / BR

Reading: *Read a Literary Passage*

ELD Standards Record Sheet

Teacher: _____ **Class:** _____

Standards: *PI.B.7*

Guided Activities and Proficiency Levels:

Students:	#1	#2	#3	#4	#5
	EM / EX / BR	EM / EX / BR	EM / EX / BR	EM / EX / BR	EM / EX / BR
	EM / EX / BR	EM / EX / BR	EM / EX / BR	EM / EX / BR	EM / EX / BR
	EM / EX / BR	EM / EX / BR	EM / EX / BR	EM / EX / BR	EM / EX / BR
	EM / EX / BR	EM / EX / BR	EM / EX / BR	EM / EX / BR	EM / EX / BR
	EM / EX / BR	EM / EX / BR	EM / EX / BR	EM / EX / BR	EM / EX / BR
	EM / EX / BR	EM / EX / BR	EM / EX / BR	EM / EX / BR	EM / EX / BR
	EM / EX / BR	EM / EX / BR	EM / EX / BR	EM / EX / BR	EM / EX / BR
	EM / EX / BR	EM / EX / BR	EM / EX / BR	EM / EX / BR	EM / EX / BR
	EM / EX / BR	EM / EX / BR	EM / EX / BR	EM / EX / BR	EM / EX / BR
	EM / EX / BR	EM / EX / BR	EM / EX / BR	EM / EX / BR	EM / EX / BR
	EM / EX / BR	EM / EX / BR	EM / EX / BR	EM / EX / BR	EM / EX / BR
	EM / EX / BR	EM / EX / BR	EM / EX / BR	EM / EX / BR	EM / EX / BR
	EM / EX / BR	EM / EX / BR	EM / EX / BR	EM / EX / BR	EM / EX / BR
	EM / EX / BR	EM / EX / BR	EM / EX / BR	EM / EX / BR	EM / EX / BR
	EM / EX / BR	EM / EX / BR	EM / EX / BR	EM / EX / BR	EM / EX / BR
	EM / EX / BR	EM / EX / BR	EM / EX / BR	EM / EX / BR	EM / EX / BR
	EM / EX / BR	EM / EX / BR	EM / EX / BR	EM / EX / BR	EM / EX / BR
	EM / EX / BR	EM / EX / BR	EM / EX / BR	EM / EX / BR	EM / EX / BR
	EM / EX / BR	EM / EX / BR	EM / EX / BR	EM / EX / BR	EM / EX / BR

Reading: *Read a Literary Passage*

ELD Standards Record Sheet

Teacher: _____ **Class:** _____

Standards: *PI.B.8*

Guided Activities and Proficiency Levels:

Students:	#1	#2	#3	#4	#5
	EM / EX / BR	EM / EX / BR	EM / EX / BR	EM / EX / BR	EM / EX / BR
	EM / EX / BR	EM / EX / BR	EM / EX / BR	EM / EX / BR	EM / EX / BR
	EM / EX / BR	EM / EX / BR	EM / EX / BR	EM / EX / BR	EM / EX / BR
	EM / EX / BR	EM / EX / BR	EM / EX / BR	EM / EX / BR	EM / EX / BR
	EM / EX / BR	EM / EX / BR	EM / EX / BR	EM / EX / BR	EM / EX / BR
	EM / EX / BR	EM / EX / BR	EM / EX / BR	EM / EX / BR	EM / EX / BR
	EM / EX / BR	EM / EX / BR	EM / EX / BR	EM / EX / BR	EM / EX / BR
	EM / EX / BR	EM / EX / BR	EM / EX / BR	EM / EX / BR	EM / EX / BR
	EM / EX / BR	EM / EX / BR	EM / EX / BR	EM / EX / BR	EM / EX / BR
	EM / EX / BR	EM / EX / BR	EM / EX / BR	EM / EX / BR	EM / EX / BR
	EM / EX / BR	EM / EX / BR	EM / EX / BR	EM / EX / BR	EM / EX / BR
	EM / EX / BR	EM / EX / BR	EM / EX / BR	EM / EX / BR	EM / EX / BR
	EM / EX / BR	EM / EX / BR	EM / EX / BR	EM / EX / BR	EM / EX / BR
	EM / EX / BR	EM / EX / BR	EM / EX / BR	EM / EX / BR	EM / EX / BR
	EM / EX / BR	EM / EX / BR	EM / EX / BR	EM / EX / BR	EM / EX / BR
	EM / EX / BR	EM / EX / BR	EM / EX / BR	EM / EX / BR	EM / EX / BR
	EM / EX / BR	EM / EX / BR	EM / EX / BR	EM / EX / BR	EM / EX / BR
	EM / EX / BR	EM / EX / BR	EM / EX / BR	EM / EX / BR	EM / EX / BR
	EM / EX / BR	EM / EX / BR	EM / EX / BR	EM / EX / BR	EM / EX / BR

Reading: *Read a Literary Passage*

ELD Standards Record Sheet

Teacher: _____ **Class:** _____

Standards: *PII.A.1*

Guided Activities and Proficiency Levels:

Students:	#1	#2	#3	#4	#5
_____	EM / EX / BR	EM / EX / BR	EM / EX / BR	EM / EX / BR	EM / EX / BR
_____	EM / EX / BR	EM / EX / BR	EM / EX / BR	EM / EX / BR	EM / EX / BR
_____	EM / EX / BR	EM / EX / BR	EM / EX / BR	EM / EX / BR	EM / EX / BR
_____	EM / EX / BR	EM / EX / BR	EM / EX / BR	EM / EX / BR	EM / EX / BR
_____	EM / EX / BR	EM / EX / BR	EM / EX / BR	EM / EX / BR	EM / EX / BR
_____	EM / EX / BR	EM / EX / BR	EM / EX / BR	EM / EX / BR	EM / EX / BR
_____	EM / EX / BR	EM / EX / BR	EM / EX / BR	EM / EX / BR	EM / EX / BR
_____	EM / EX / BR	EM / EX / BR	EM / EX / BR	EM / EX / BR	EM / EX / BR
_____	EM / EX / BR	EM / EX / BR	EM / EX / BR	EM / EX / BR	EM / EX / BR
_____	EM / EX / BR	EM / EX / BR	EM / EX / BR	EM / EX / BR	EM / EX / BR
_____	EM / EX / BR	EM / EX / BR	EM / EX / BR	EM / EX / BR	EM / EX / BR
_____	EM / EX / BR	EM / EX / BR	EM / EX / BR	EM / EX / BR	EM / EX / BR
_____	EM / EX / BR	EM / EX / BR	EM / EX / BR	EM / EX / BR	EM / EX / BR
_____	EM / EX / BR	EM / EX / BR	EM / EX / BR	EM / EX / BR	EM / EX / BR
_____	EM / EX / BR	EM / EX / BR	EM / EX / BR	EM / EX / BR	EM / EX / BR
_____	EM / EX / BR	EM / EX / BR	EM / EX / BR	EM / EX / BR	EM / EX / BR
_____	EM / EX / BR	EM / EX / BR	EM / EX / BR	EM / EX / BR	EM / EX / BR
_____	EM / EX / BR	EM / EX / BR	EM / EX / BR	EM / EX / BR	EM / EX / BR
_____	EM / EX / BR	EM / EX / BR	EM / EX / BR	EM / EX / BR	EM / EX / BR
_____	EM / EX / BR	EM / EX / BR	EM / EX / BR	EM / EX / BR	EM / EX / BR

ELD Standards Record Sheet

Teacher: _____ **Class:** _____

Standards: *PII.A.2*   **Guided Activities and Proficiency Levels:**

Students:	#1	#2	#3	#4	#5
	EM / EX / BR	EM / EX / BR	EM / EX / BR	EM / EX / BR	EM / EX / BR
	EM / EX / BR	EM / EX / BR	EM / EX / BR	EM / EX / BR	EM / EX / BR
	EM / EX / BR	EM / EX / BR	EM / EX / BR	EM / EX / BR	EM / EX / BR
	EM / EX / BR	EM / EX / BR	EM / EX / BR	EM / EX / BR	EM / EX / BR
	EM / EX / BR	EM / EX / BR	EM / EX / BR	EM / EX / BR	EM / EX / BR
	EM / EX / BR	EM / EX / BR	EM / EX / BR	EM / EX / BR	EM / EX / BR
	EM / EX / BR	EM / EX / BR	EM / EX / BR	EM / EX / BR	EM / EX / BR
	EM / EX / BR	EM / EX / BR	EM / EX / BR	EM / EX / BR	EM / EX / BR
	EM / EX / BR	EM / EX / BR	EM / EX / BR	EM / EX / BR	EM / EX / BR
	EM / EX / BR	EM / EX / BR	EM / EX / BR	EM / EX / BR	EM / EX / BR
	EM / EX / BR	EM / EX / BR	EM / EX / BR	EM / EX / BR	EM / EX / BR
	EM / EX / BR	EM / EX / BR	EM / EX / BR	EM / EX / BR	EM / EX / BR
	EM / EX / BR	EM / EX / BR	EM / EX / BR	EM / EX / BR	EM / EX / BR
	EM / EX / BR	EM / EX / BR	EM / EX / BR	EM / EX / BR	EM / EX / BR
	EM / EX / BR	EM / EX / BR	EM / EX / BR	EM / EX / BR	EM / EX / BR
	EM / EX / BR	EM / EX / BR	EM / EX / BR	EM / EX / BR	EM / EX / BR
	EM / EX / BR	EM / EX / BR	EM / EX / BR	EM / EX / BR	EM / EX / BR
	EM / EX / BR	EM / EX / BR	EM / EX / BR	EM / EX / BR	EM / EX / BR
	EM / EX / BR	EM / EX / BR	EM / EX / BR	EM / EX / BR	EM / EX / BR

Practice Activity #1

Name: ···

Directions: Practice reading the story aloud:

☐ To myself   ☐ With a partner   ☐ With an adult

Directions: Cut out and match each picture to the story.

	Oscar was excited for class today. His teacher had told the students to bring in something for show and tell. Oscar wanted to share the trophy that he and his basketball team had won.
	"Can I bring this in for show and tell today?" Oscar asked his mom.
	"Of course, dear!" replied his mom.

	In class, Oscar anxiously waited for his turn to share. He enjoyed seeing all of the cool things that his classmates had brought in.
	"Okay, next up we have, Oscar," said his teacher.
	Taking a deep breath, Oscar suddenly felt too nervous to move. He stood up holding his trophy, but he didn't go up to the front.

	"Oscar? Are you okay?" asked his teacher.
	Hearing his teacher's voice snapped Oscar out of his frozen state. He looked around and felt relieved to see his classmates smiling at him.
	"Yes, I'm okay," replied Oscar. He walked to the front of the class and proceeded to proudly share his trophy. When he was done, everyone gave a loud round of applause.

✂    ✂    ✂

Practice Activity #1

Name:

Directions: Answer the following questions about the story. Write complete sentences and use the text to help you.

1 | **WHO** is the story about?

2 | **WHERE** does the story take place?

3 | **WHAT** happens in the story?

Practice Activity #2

Name: ....

Directions: Practice reading the story aloud:

☐ To myself   ☐ With a partner   ☐ With an adult

Directions: Cut out and match each picture to the story.

	Anila was sick so she had to stay home from school. She was disappointed because it was her best friend's, Trisha, birthday. "I had made her a birthday card, but now I can't give it to her," Anila sadly thought to herself. She wished that she could be at school celebrating with her friend.
	Just then there was a knock on her door. "Anila, how are you feeling, sweetheart?" asked her father as he came into the room. He placed a bowl of soup on her nightstand. "I'm feeling a little better, but I'm sad that I didn't get to give Trisha her birthday card," Anila solemnly replied.
	"I figured you'd be disappointed about that," said her father. "So I asked Trisha's mom if you both can talk online for awhile." Anila immediately felt excited. "Oh, thank you dad!" After her dad set up the laptop, Anila talked to her friend online for a while. She wished Trisha a happy birthday and showed her the card. Trisha said she loved it and couldn't wait until Anila felt better.

Practice Activity #2

Name: ....

Directions: Answer the following questions about the story. Write complete sentences and use the text to help you.
....

| 1 | **WHO** is the story about?

_____

_____

_____

| 2 | **WHERE** does the story take place?

_____

_____

_____

| 3 | **WHAT** happens in the story?

_____

_____

_____

_____

Practice Activity #3

Name: ....

Directions: Practice reading the story aloud:

☐ To myself   ☐ With a partner   ☐ With an adult

Directions: Cut out and match each picture to the story.

	One day, David was in his front yard fixing his bike. He was working on the tires when he heard a soft sound come from the bushes nearby. "What was that?" David thought to himself. He heard the sound again and went over to the bushes where it was coming from. David stayed still and listened again.
	When he heard the sound again, David pushed the leaves and branches aside. "A kitten?" David exclaimed as peered down at a tiny kitten huddled in the bushes. "How'd you get in here?" The little kitten looked up at David and softly meowed as he carefully picked it up.
	The kitten had no tag or collar. "You must be all alone and hungry," David said as he gently placed the kitten onto a blanket. He ran into the house and poured a small bowl of milk. When he returned he placed the bowl in front of the kitten. He watched as the kitten drank the entire bowl of milk with its tiny tongue. David decide that he would ask his parents if he could keep it as his new pet.

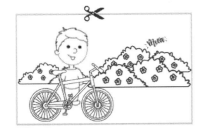

Practice Activity #3

Name: ....

Directions: Answer the following questions about the story. Write complete sentences and use the text to help you.

1 **WHO** is the story about?

2 **WHERE** does the story take place?

3 **WHAT** happens in the story?

Practice Activity #4

Name: ....

Directions: Practice reading the story aloud:

☐ To myself   ☐ With a partner   ☐ With an adult

Directions: Cut out and match each picture to the story.

	Vanessa was feeling sad. She had lost her favorite teddy bear a week ago. "It's okay, honey," comforted her mom as they sat at the table eating breakfast. "I'm sure you'll find your teddy bear soon." Vanessa just quietly nodded and continued to eat her breakfast. She really missed her favorite companion.
	"Tell you what, how about we finish our breakfast and watch a movie together in the living room?" Vanessa's mom suggested. "Sounds good, mom," replied Vanessa. She helped her mom clear the table and wash the dishes. Then they both went into the living room where Vanessa noticed a box on the floor.
	"What's in the box?" Vanessa asked her mom. "I don't know, why don't you open it," her mom said. Vanessa sat down on the rug and opened the box. It was her teddy bear! Vanessa gave it a big hug. "I found it under the seat in the car," said her mom. Vanessa gave her mom a big hug too.

Practice Activity #4

Name: ....

Directions: Answer the following questions about the story. Write complete sentences and use the text to help you.

1 **WHO** is the story about?

2 **WHERE** does the story take place?

3 **WHAT** happens in the story?

Practice Activity #5

Name:

Directions: Practice reading the story aloud:

☐ To myself ☐ With a partner ☐ With an adult

Directions: Cut out and match each picture to the story.

	It was the first day at a new school. Lawrence was nervous because he didn't know anyone. "Don't worry, you'll make new friends in no time," his mother had said to him when she had dropped him off in the morning. Unsure if what she said was true, Lawrence quickly walked down the hallway towards class.
	As he rounded a corner, his backpack had not been zipped closed all the way and a few of his books fell on to the floor. "Ugh, great!" Lawrence muttered to himself as he bent down to pick up his books. "Hey, need some help there?" Lawrence heard a voice asked. He looked up to see a girl starting to help him pick up his books.
	"I'm Rachel by the way," said the girl. "It's nice to meet you." After picking up all the books and standing back up, Lawrence replied, "Hey, thanks for the help. I'm Lawrence. Nice to meet you, too." Lawrence found out that they were in the same class. As they walked together into class Lawrence felt a little better.

Practice Activity #5

Name:

Directions: Answer the following questions about the story. Write complete sentences and use the text to help you.

1 **WHO** is the story about?

2 **WHERE** does the story take place?

3 **WHAT** happens in the story?

Reading
Read an Informational Passage

This section includes:
- Guided Activities
- Teacher's ELD Standards Record Sheet
- Student Practice Activities:
  - Informational passage practice activities

Alignment to CA ELD Standards: **Alignment to CCSS:**

Part I: Interacting in Meaningful Ways

B.6 Reading/viewing closely

Reading closely literary and informational   RL.2.1–7, 9–10; RI.2.1–7,
texts and viewing multimedia to determine   9–10; SL.2.2–3; L.2.3, 4,
how meaning is conveyed explicitly and   6
implicitly through language

Part I: Interacting in Meaningful Ways

B.7 Evaluating language choices

Evaluating how well writers and speakers   RL.2.3–4, 6; RI.2.2, 6, 8;
use language to support ideas and opinions   SL.2.3; L.2.3–6
with details or reasons depending on
modality, text type, purpose, audience,
topic, and content area

Part I: Interacting in Meaningful Ways

B.8 Analyzing language choice

Analyzing how writers and speakers use   RL.2.4–5; RI.2.4–5;
vocabulary and other language resources   SL.2.3; L.2.3–6
for specific purposes (to explain, persuade,
entertain, etc.) depending on modality, text
type, purpose, audience, topic, and content
area

Reading
Read an Informational Passage

- -

Alignment to CA ELD Standards:

Alignment to CCSS:

Part II: Learning About How English Works
 A.1 Structuring Cohesive Texts
 Understanding text structure

RL.2.5; RI.2.5; W.2.1–5; SL.2.4

Part II: Learning About How English Works
 A.2 Structuring Cohesive Texts
 Understanding Cohesion

RL.2.5; RI.2.5; W.2.1–4; SL.2.4; L.2.1, 3

- -

Guided Activities Direction:

1. Show students the informational passage, pictures, and questions.
2. Follow the teacher directions.
3. **Say** the **Teacher Script** (indicated by)
4. Guide students through:
   - Reading the text independently
   - Comprehending the text
   - Associating the pictures with the text
   - Answering basic comprehension questions
5. Review the questions and answers with the students. (questions are indicated by ⬛ **1**)
6. Then have students practice with additional sheets.

Guided Activity #1

 SAY   Show students the passage and questions.
Now you are going to read a text on your own and then answer the questions.

A very special place is located in the US state of Arizona. It is the Grand Canyon. The Grand Canyon is a national park. A national park is a natural park that is protected by the government.

The canyon was carved a long time ago by the Colorado River. The rushing waters of the river helped create the really tall canyon walls. Some of the rocks are millions of years old! You can actually see the different layers of rock and dirt in the canyon walls. It is like looking at a natural history book in real life.

The Grand Canyon is almost a mile deep in some places! It is over 275 miles long! It is a popular place for many visitors. Millions of people visit every year. Many people have hiked down to the bottom of the canyon.

A diverse number of animals live in The Grand Canyon. Squirrels and bighorn sheep can be seen perched along the edges of the canyon cliffs. Large birds can be seen soaring through the canyon also.

1   **What is the main idea of the text?**

   A. national parks

   B. Grand Canyon

   C. Arizona

2   **What helped create the canyon?**

  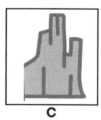

   A   **B**   **C**

3   **What kinds of animals can be found living there?**

   A. squirrels and bighorn sheep

   B. squirrels and polar bears

   C. bighorn sheep and lions

103

Guided Activity #1

A very special place is located in the US state of Arizona. It is the Grand Canyon. The Grand Canyon is a national park. A national park is a natural park that is protected by the government.

The canyon was carved a long time ago by the Colorado River. The rushing waters of the river helped create the really tall canyon walls. Some of the rocks are millions of years old! You can actually see the different layers of rock and dirt in the canyon walls. It is like looking at a natural history book in real life.

The Grand Canyon is almost a mile deep in some places! It is over 275 miles long! It is a popular place for many visitors. Millions of people visit every year. Many people have hiked down to the bottom of the canyon.

A diverse number of animals live in The Grand Canyon. Squirrels and bighorn sheep can be seen perched along the edges of the canyon cliffs. Large birds can be seen soaring through the canyon also.

Guided Activity #1

Now have the students read and answer the questions for the passage. Guide the students through answering the comprehension questions by using both the pictures and sentences of the story.

· ·

1 **What is the main idea of the text?**

    A. national parks

    B. Grand Canyon

    C. Arizona

· ·

2 **What helped create the canyon?**

 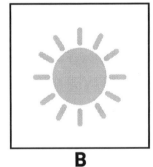 

    A   **B**   **C**

· ·

3 **What kinds of animals can be found living there?**

    A. squirrels and bighorn sheep

    B. squirrels and polar bears

    C. bighorn sheep and lions

Guided Activity #2

SAY Show students the passage and questions.

Now you are going to read a text on your own. I will then ask you some questions about what you read.

Egypt is a country located in northern Africa. Egypt is home to an ancient civilization, or advanced group of people, who built amazing things. They built some of the world's largest structures called pyramids. These pyramids were built a long time ago.

Pyramids were built for the kings. They were built as the resting place for kings who passed away. The large pyramids were mostly built of limestone which was a hard sedimentary rock. The bottom of the pyramid was usually always a perfect square.

The pyramids had a lot of secret rooms and chambers. The rooms contained plenty of valuable treasures and artifacts. The Egyptians also had their own kind of writing on the walls of the pyramids called hieroglyphs.

The pyramids of Egypt are a popular place for visitors. People who study the pyramids are still learning new things today. There is a lot of history that can be found at the pyramids.

1 **What is the main idea of the text?**

A. how to build pyramids

B. pyramids in Mexico

C. pyramids in Egypt

2 **Which shape is usually the bottom of a pyramid?**

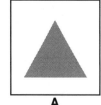

A   B   C

3 **Why were the pyramids built?**

A. to show how big they are

B. for the kings

C. as homes for animals

106

Guided Activity #2

Egypt is a country located in northern Africa. Egypt is home to an ancient civilization, or advanced group of people, who built amazing things. They built some of the world's largest structures called pyramids. These pyramids were built a long time ago.

Pyramids were built for the kings. They were built as the resting place for kings who passed away. The large pyramids were mostly built of limestone which was a hard sedimentary rock. The bottom of the pyramid was usually always a perfect square.

The pyramids had a lot of secret rooms and chambers. The rooms contained plenty of valuable treasures and artifacts. The Egyptians also had their own kind of writing on the walls of the pyramids called hieroglyphs.

The pyramids of Egypt are a popular place for visitors. People who study the pyramids are still learning new things today. There is a lot of history that can be found at the pyramids.

Guided Activity #2

Now have the students read and answer the questions for the passage. Guide the students through answering the comprehension questions by using both the pictures and sentences of the story.

· ·

1 **What is the main idea of the text?**

   A. how to build pyramids

   B. pyramids in Mexico

   C. pyramids in Egypt

· ·

2 **Which shape is usually the bottom of a pyramid?**

  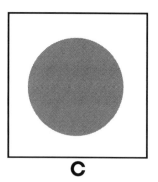

   A   **B**   **C**

· ·

3 **Why were the pyramids built?**

   A. to show how big they are

   B. for the kings

   C. as homes for animals

Guided Activity #3

 SAY Show students the passage and questions.
Now you are going to read a text on your own. I will then ask you some questions about what you read.

Galileo Galilei was a famous astronomer in history. He lived in the late 1500s to the early 1600s. He studied the planets and stars and was known as the "father of observational astronomy".

He used a telescope to observe the night sky. A telescope helps people see far away objects up close. Galileo famously observed that the planet Jupiter had four large moons.

He also discovered that the sun had dark areas called sunspots. He also observed that the Earth's moon had tall hills and deep valleys on the surface.

However, the church back then did not agree with Galileo's work. They didn't believe the same thing as he did. Questioned for his findings, Galileo eventually was put under house arrest.

Galileo's work and findings are still celebrated today. Astronomers and scientists are still learning more about the planet and stars!

1 **What is the main idea of the text?**

   A. Galileo Galilei

   B. The Catholic Church

   C. telescopes

2 **Which planet did Galileo see had 4 moons?**

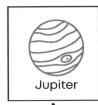 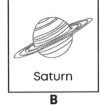 

Jupiter	Saturn	Earth
A	**B**	**C**

3 **What does a telescope do?**

   A. helps you to call someone faraway

   B. helps you to see across the table

   C. helps you to see faraway objects up close

109

Guided Activity #3

Galileo Galilei was a famous astronomer in history. He lived in the late 1500s to the early 1600s. He studied the planets and stars and was known as the "father of observational astronomy".

He used a telescope to observe the night sky. A telescope helps people see far away objects up close. Galileo famously observed that the planet Jupiter had four large moons.

He also discovered that the sun had dark areas called sunspots. He also observed that the Earth's moon had tall hills and deep valleys on the surface.

However, the church back then did not agree with Galileo's work. They didn't believe the same thing as he did. Questioned for his findings, Galileo eventually was put under house arrest.

Galileo's work and findings are still celebrated today. Astronomers and scientists are still learning more about the planet and stars!

Guided Activity #3

Now have the students read and answer the questions for the passage. Guide the students through answering the comprehension questions by using both the pictures and sentences of the story.

• •

1 **What is the main idea of the text?**

　　A. Galileo Galilei

　　B. The Catholic Church

　　C. telescopes

• •

2 **Which planet did Galileo see had 4 moons?**

 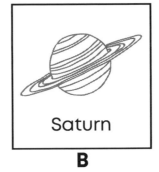 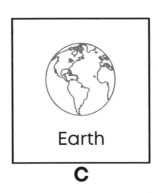

Jupiter	Saturn	Earth
A	**B**	**C**

• •

3 **What does a telescope do?**

　　A. helps you to call someone faraway

　　B. helps you to see across the table

　　C. helps you to see faraway objects up close

Guided Activity #4

 SAY Show students the passage and questions.

Now you are going to read a text on your own. I will then ask you some questions about what you read.

Do you know about sharks? Sharks are a species of fish that can be found living in the deep oceans. A lot of people are afraid of these wonderful animals. Their fear comes from the lack of information and understanding as well as seeing how sharks are portrayed as attacking people in movies.

There are over 350 different kinds of sharks. The great white and hammerhead sharks are well known.

Sharks come in different sizes. Most of them have long thin bodies with skin that feels like sandpaper. They also have powerful jaws with sharp teeth. Their sense of smell is also very good. They have a powerful tail that helps propel them through the water.

Sharks hunt and eat fish, marine mammals, and other sea creatures. Many people think that sharks bite people on purpose, but that is not true. Sharks mistaken a swimming person for one of their prey.

Learning more about these animals can keep both them and people safe!

1 **What is the main idea of the text?**

    A. marine animals

    B. sharks

    C. ocean safety

2 **What is one type of shark?**

 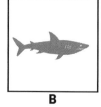 

    A   **B**   **C**

3 **What does a shark eat?**

    A. fish and other marine animals

    B. seaweed and kelp

    C. coral reefs

Guided Activity #4

Do you know about sharks? Sharks are a species of fish that can be found living in the deep oceans. A lot of people are afraid of these wonderful animals. Their fear comes from the lack of information and understanding as well as seeing how sharks are portrayed as attacking people in movies.

There are over 350 different kinds of sharks. The great white and hammerhead sharks are well known.

Sharks come in different sizes. Most of them have long thin bodies with skin that feels like sandpaper. They also have powerful jaws with sharp teeth. Their sense of smell is also very good. They have a powerful tail that helps propel them through the water.

Sharks hunt and eat fish, marine mammals, and other sea creatures. Many people think that sharks bite people on purpose, but that is not true. Sharks mistaken a swimming person for one of their prey.

Learning more about these animals can keep both them and people safe!

Guided Activity #4

Now have the students read and answer the questions for the passage. Guide the students through answering the comprehension questions by using both the pictures and sentences of the story.

• •

1 | **What is the main idea?**

  A. marine animals

  B. sharks

  C. ocean safety

• •

2 | **What is one type of shark?**

 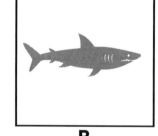 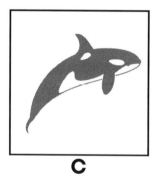

  A   **B**   **C**

• •

3 | **What does a shark eat?**

  A. fish and other marine animals

  B. seaweed and kelp

  C. coral reefs

Guided Activity #5

 SAY Show students the passage and questions.
Now you are going to read a text on your own. I will then ask you some questions about what you read.

Do you know what an avalanche is? An avalanche is when too much snow on a mountain falls down the mountainside. Avalanches can be very dangerous. They can happen anywhere and at anytime without warning.

When this happens, a large amount of snow slides down the mountain quickly. Being in the path of an avalanche is very dangerous. Sometimes big rocks, dirt, and even trees are carried down with the snow. Different things can trigger an avalanche, such as an earthquake or even humans skiing down the mountain.

Some people get caught in an avalanche. They are usually skiers and other people who are in the path. Some people get buried under the heavy snow and need help right away! Emergency workers are trained to save people trapped in an avalanche.

Avalanches are dangerous and can occur without warning. It is important to stay safe and know what to do when it happens.

1 **What is the main idea of the text?**

A. avalanches

B. how snow is formed

C. mountains

2 **What is sometimes carried down in an avalanche?**

 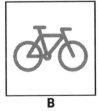 

A   B   C

3 **Why are avalanches so dangerous?**

A. the mountains will no longer have snow

B. people can become buried in them

C. they melt into water

115

Guided Activity #5

Do you know what an avalanche is? An avalanche is when too much snow on a mountain falls down the mountainside. Avalanches can be very dangerous. They can happen anywhere and at anytime without warning.

When this happens, a large amount of snow slides down the mountain quickly. Being in the path of an avalanche is very dangerous. Sometimes big rocks, dirt, and even trees are carried down with the snow. Different things can trigger an avalanche, such as an earthquake or even humans skiing down the mountain.

Some people get caught in an avalanche. They are usually skiers and other people who are in the path. Some people get buried under the heavy snow and need help right away! Emergency workers are trained to save people trapped in an avalanche.

Avalanches are dangerous and can occur without warning. It is important to stay safe and know what to do when it happens.

Guided Activity #5

Now have the students read and answer the questions for the passage. Guide the students through answering the comprehension questions by using both the pictures and sentences of the story.

1 ## What is the main idea of the text?

    A. avalanches

    B. how snow is formed

    C. mountains

2 ## What is sometimes carried down in an avalanche?

 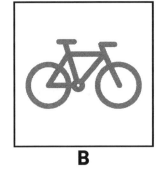 

    A   **B**   **C**

3 ## Why are avalanches so dangerous?

    A. the mountains will no longer have snow

    B. people can become buried in them

    C. they melt into water

Reading: *Read an Informational Passage*

ELD Standards Record Sheet

Directions:

1. Look at the CA ELD standards (**BELOW**) that correspond to this section.
2. Reference these specific standards for the template Record Sheet.
3. Use the following template Record Sheet to monitor students' proficiency levels for the **GUIDED ACTIVITIES** in this section.
4. Fill out all the information. Circle, check, highlight the proficiency level. (*There is space for 20 students. Make additional copies, as needed*)
5. Retain for your records to be used during grading, parent/student conferences, lesson planning, ELD documentation, etc.

 Suggestion: You can make one copy of each guided activity and/or the student practice sheets and laminate them. Organize the laminated sheets onto a book ring. Now it'll be easily accessible for whole group, small group, one-on-one, centers, etc. Copy as many of the ELD Standards Record Sheet as you need and keep it handy along with the activities.

CA ELD Standards & Proficiency Levels
Part I: Interacting in Meaningful Ways
B.6 Reading/viewing closely

EMERGING (EM)	EXPANDING (EX)	BRIDGING (BR)
*Requires **Substantial** Support*	*Requires **Moderate** Support*	*Requires **Light** Support*

• Describes:
  ◦ Ideas
  ◦ phenomena (e.g., plant life cycle)
  ◦ text elements (e.g. main idea,
• characters, events)
• Reads and comprehends a select set of grade-level texts and multimedia with:
  ◦ Simple sentences
  ◦ Familiar vocabulary
  ◦ Support by graphics or pictures
• Requires substantial support
	• Describes in <u>greater details</u>:
	  ◦ Ideas
	  ◦ phenomena (e.g., how earthworms eat)
	  ◦ text elements (e.g. setting, events)
	• Reads and comprehends a <u>variety of</u> grade-level texts and multimedia with:
	  ◦ <u>Reliance on content and prior</u>
	• <u>knowledge to obtain meaning from print</u>
	  ◦ Support by graphics or pictures
	• Requires <u>moderate</u> support
		• Describes <u>using key details</u>:
		  ◦ Ideas
		  ◦ phenomena (e.g., erosion)
		  ◦ text elements (e.g. central message, character traits)
		• Reads and comprehends a variety of grade-level texts and multimedia with:
		  ◦ <u>Limited comprehension difficulty</u>
		  ◦ <u>Comprehension of concrete and abstract topics</u>
		  ◦ <u>Recognize language subtleties</u>
		  ◦ Support by graphics or pictures
		• Requires <u>light</u> support

ELD Standards Record Sheet

CA ELD Standards & Proficiency Levels
Part I: Interacting in Meaningful Ways
B.7 Evaluating Language Choices

EMERGING (EM) ➤	EXPANDING (EX) ➤	BRIDGING (BR) ➤
*Requires **Substantial** Support*	*Requires **Moderate** Support*	*Requires **Light** Support*
• Describe the language writers or speakers use to present an idea:(e.g. the words and phrases used to describe a character) • Requires prompting and substantial support	• Describe the language writers or speakers use to present or <u>support</u> an idea: (e.g. the author's choice of vocabulary or phrasing to portray characters, places, or real people) • Requires prompting and <u>moderate</u> support	• Describe <u>how well writers or speakers use specific language resources to support an opinion</u> or present an idea: (e.g. whether the vocabulary used to present evidence is strong enough) • Requires prompting and <u>light</u> support

CA ELD Standards & Proficiency Levels
Part I: Interacting in Meaningful Ways
B.8 Analyzing Language Choices

EMERGING (EM) ➤	EXPANDING (EX) ➤	BRIDGING (BR) ➤
*Requires **Substantial** Support*	*Requires **Moderate** Support*	*Requires **Light** Support*
• Distinguish how two different frequently used words: (e.g. describing a character as happy vs. angry) • Produce a different effect on the audience	• Distinguish how two different words <u>with similar meaning</u>: (e.g. describing a character as happy vs ecstatic) • Produce <u>shades of meaning</u> and a different effect on the audience	• Distinguish how <u>multiple</u> different words with similar meaning: (e.g. pleased vs happy vs ecstatic, heard vs knew vs believed) • Produce shades of meaning and a different effect on the audience

ELD Standards Record Sheet

CA ELD Standards & Proficiency Levels
Part II: Learning About How English Works
A.1 Understanding text structure

EMERGING (EM)	EXPANDING (EX)	BRIDGING (BR)
*Requires **Substantial** Support*	*Requires **Moderate** Support*	*Requires **Light** Support*
• *Apply understanding of how text types are organized to express ideas (e.g. how a story is organized sequentially)* • *Comprehend & compose texts with substantial support* • *Comprehend & write texts in shared language activities (guided by teacher, peers, and sometimes independently)*	• *Apply understanding of how <u>different</u> text types are organized to express ideas (e.g. how a story is organized sequentially with predictable stages vs how an information report is organized by topic and details)* • *Comprehend & write texts (w/ <u>increasing independence</u>)*	• *Apply understanding of how different text types are organized <u>predictably</u> to express ideas (e.g. a narrative vs an informative/explanatory text vs an opinion text)* • *Comprehend & write texts (<u>independently</u>)*

CA ELD Standards & Proficiency Levels
Part II: Learning About How English Works
A.2 Understanding cohesion

EMERGING (EM)	EXPANDING (EX)	BRIDGING (BR)
*Requires **Substantial** Support*	*Requires **Moderate** Support*	*Requires **Light** Support*
• *Apply basic understanding of how ideas, events, or reasons are linked throughout a text* • *Uses more everyday connecting words or phrases (e.g. today, then)* • *Comprehend & write texts in shared language activities (guided by teacher, peers, and sometimes independently)*	• *Apply understanding of how ideas, events, or reasons are linked throughout a text* • *Uses a <u>growing number</u> of connecting words or phrases (e.g. after a long time, first/next)* • *Comprehend & write texts (w/ <u>increasing independence</u>)*	• *Apply understanding of how ideas, events, or reasons are linked throughout a text* • *Uses a <u>variety</u> of connecting words or phrases (e.g. for example, after that, suddenly)* • *Comprehend & write texts (<u>independently</u>)*

Reading: *Read an Informational Passage*

ELD Standards Record Sheet

Teacher: _____ **Class:** _____

Standards: *PI.B.6* **Guided Activities and Proficiency Levels:**

Students:	#1	#2	#3	#4	#5
	EM / EX / BR	EM / EX / BR	EM / EX / BR	EM / EX / BR	EM / EX / BR
	EM / EX / BR	EM / EX / BR	EM / EX / BR	EM / EX / BR	EM / EX / BR
	EM / EX / BR	EM / EX / BR	EM / EX / BR	EM / EX / BR	EM / EX / BR
	EM / EX / BR	EM / EX / BR	EM / EX / BR	EM / EX / BR	EM / EX / BR
	EM / EX / BR	EM / EX / BR	EM / EX / BR	EM / EX / BR	EM / EX / BR
	EM / EX / BR	EM / EX / BR	EM / EX / BR	EM / EX / BR	EM / EX / BR
	EM / EX / BR	EM / EX / BR	EM / EX / BR	EM / EX / BR	EM / EX / BR
	EM / EX / BR	EM / EX / BR	EM / EX / BR	EM / EX / BR	EM / EX / BR
	EM / EX / BR	EM / EX / BR	EM / EX / BR	EM / EX / BR	EM / EX / BR
	EM / EX / BR	EM / EX / BR	EM / EX / BR	EM / EX / BR	EM / EX / BR
	EM / EX / BR	EM / EX / BR	EM / EX / BR	EM / EX / BR	EM / EX / BR
	EM / EX / BR	EM / EX / BR	EM / EX / BR	EM / EX / BR	EM / EX / BR
	EM / EX / BR	EM / EX / BR	EM / EX / BR	EM / EX / BR	EM / EX / BR
	EM / EX / BR	EM / EX / BR	EM / EX / BR	EM / EX / BR	EM / EX / BR
	EM / EX / BR	EM / EX / BR	EM / EX / BR	EM / EX / BR	EM / EX / BR
	EM / EX / BR	EM / EX / BR	EM / EX / BR	EM / EX / BR	EM / EX / BR
	EM / EX / BR	EM / EX / BR	EM / EX / BR	EM / EX / BR	EM / EX / BR
	EM / EX / BR	EM / EX / BR	EM / EX / BR	EM / EX / BR	EM / EX / BR
	EM / EX / BR	EM / EX / BR	EM / EX / BR	EM / EX / BR	EM / EX / BR

ELD Standards Record Sheet

Teacher: _____ **Class:** _____

Standards: *PI.B.7*   **Guided Activities and Proficiency Levels:**

Students:	#1	#2	#3	#4	#5
_____	EM / EX / BR	EM / EX / BR	EM / EX / BR	EM / EX / BR	EM / EX / BR
_____	EM / EX / BR	EM / EX / BR	EM / EX / BR	EM / EX / BR	EM / EX / BR
_____	EM / EX / BR	EM / EX / BR	EM / EX / BR	EM / EX / BR	EM / EX / BR
_____	EM / EX / BR	EM / EX / BR	EM / EX / BR	EM / EX / BR	EM / EX / BR
_____	EM / EX / BR	EM / EX / BR	EM / EX / BR	EM / EX / BR	EM / EX / BR
_____	EM / EX / BR	EM / EX / BR	EM / EX / BR	EM / EX / BR	EM / EX / BR
_____	EM / EX / BR	EM / EX / BR	EM / EX / BR	EM / EX / BR	EM / EX / BR
_____	EM / EX / BR	EM / EX / BR	EM / EX / BR	EM / EX / BR	EM / EX / BR
_____	EM / EX / BR	EM / EX / BR	EM / EX / BR	EM / EX / BR	EM / EX / BR
_____	EM / EX / BR	EM / EX / BR	EM / EX / BR	EM / FX / BR	EM / EX / BR
_____	EM / EX / BR	EM / EX / BR	EM / EX / BR	EM / EX / BR	EM / EX / BR
_____	EM / EX / BR	EM / EX / BR	EM / EX / BR	EM / EX / BR	EM / EX / BR
_____	EM / EX / BR	EM / EX / BR	EM / EX / BR	EM / EX / BR	EM / EX / BR
_____	EM / EX / BR	EM / EX / BR	EM / EX / BR	EM / EX / BR	EM / EX / BR
_____	EM / EX / BR	EM / EX / BR	EM / EX / BR	EM / EX / BR	EM / EX / BR
_____	EM / EX / BR	EM / EX / BR	EM / EX / BR	EM / EX / BR	EM / EX / BR
_____	EM / EX / BR	EM / EX / BR	EM / EX / BR	EM / EX / BR	EM / EX / BR
_____	EM / EX / BR	EM / EX / BR	EM / EX / BR	EM / EX / BR	EM / EX / BR
_____	EM / EX / BR	EM / EX / BR	EM / EX / BR	EM / EX / BR	EM / EX / BR

Reading: *Read an Informational Passage*

ELD Standards Record Sheet

Teacher: _____ **Class:** _____

Standards: *PI.B.8*

Guided Activities and Proficiency Levels:

Students:	#1	#2	#3	#4	#5
	EM / EX / BR	EM / EX / BR	EM / EX / BR	EM / EX / BR	EM / EX / BR
	EM / EX / BR	EM / EX / BR	EM / EX / BR	EM / EX / BR	EM / EX / BR
	EM / EX / BR	EM / EX / BR	EM / EX / BR	EM / EX / BR	EM / EX / BR
	EM / EX / BR	EM / EX / BR	EM / EX / BR	EM / EX / BR	EM / EX / BR
	EM / EX / BR	EM / EX / BR	EM / EX / BR	EM / EX / BR	EM / EX / BR
	EM / EX / BR	EM / EX / BR	EM / EX / BR	EM / EX / BR	EM / EX / BR
	EM / EX / BR	EM / EX / BR	EM / EX / BR	EM / EX / BR	EM / EX / BR
	EM / EX / BR	EM / EX / BR	EM / EX / BR	EM / EX / BR	EM / EX / BR
	EM / EX / BR	EM / EX / BR	EM / EX / BR	EM / EX / BR	EM / EX / BR
	EM / EX / BR	EM / EX / BR	EM / EX / BR	EM / EX / BR	EM / EX / BR
	EM / EX / BR	EM / EX / BR	EM / EX / BR	EM / EX / BR	EM / EX / BR
	EM / EX / BR	EM / EX / BR	EM / EX / BR	EM / EX / BR	EM / EX / BR
	EM / EX / BR	EM / EX / BR	EM / EX / BR	EM / EX / BR	EM / EX / BR
	EM / EX / BR	EM / EX / BR	EM / EX / BR	EM / EX / BR	EM / EX / BR
	EM / EX / BR	EM / EX / BR	EM / EX / BR	EM / EX / BR	EM / EX / BR
	EM / EX / BR	EM / EX / BR	EM / EX / BR	EM / EX / BR	EM / EX / BR
	EM / EX / BR	EM / EX / BR	EM / EX / BR	EM / EX / BR	EM / EX / BR
	EM / EX / BR	EM / EX / BR	EM / EX / BR	EM / EX / BR	EM / EX / BR

Reading: *Read an Informational Passage*

ELD Standards Record Sheet

Teacher: _____ **Class:** _____

Standards: *PII.A.1*   **Guided Activities and Proficiency Levels:**

Students:	#1	#2	#3	#4	#5
	EM / EX / BR	EM / EX / BR	EM / EX / BR	EM / EX / BR	EM / EX / BR
	EM / EX / BR	EM / EX / BR	EM / EX / BR	EM / EX / BR	EM / EX / BR
	EM / EX / BR	EM / EX / BR	EM / EX / BR	EM / EX / BR	EM / EX / BR
	EM / EX / BR	EM / EX / BR	EM / EX / BR	EM / EX / BR	EM / EX / BR
	EM / EX / BR	EM / EX / BR	EM / EX / BR	EM / EX / BR	EM / EX / BR
	EM / EX / BR	EM / EX / BR	EM / EX / BR	EM / EX / BR	EM / EX / BR
	EM / EX / BR	EM / EX / BR	EM / EX / BR	EM / EX / BR	EM / EX / BR
	EM / EX / BR	EM / EX / BR	EM / EX / BR	EM / EX / BR	EM / EX / BR
	EM / EX / BR	EM / EX / BR	EM / EX / BR	EM / EX / BR	EM / EX / BR
	EM / EX / BR	EM / EX / BR	EM / EX / BR	EM / EX / BR	EM / EX / BR
	EM / EX BR	EM / EX / BR	EM / EX / BR	EM / EX / BR	EM / EX / BR
	EM / EX / BR	EM / EX / BR	EM / EX / BR	EM / EX / BR	EM / EX / BR
	EM / EX / BR	EM / EX / BR	EM / EX / BR	EM / EX / BR	EM / EX / BR
	EM / EX / BR	EM / EX / BR	EM / EX / BR	EM / EX / BR	EM / EX / BR
	EM / EX / BR	EM / EX / BR	EM / EX / BR	EM / EX / BR	EM / EX / BR
	EM / EX / BR	EM / EX / BR	EM / EX / BR	EM / EX / BR	EM / EX / BR
	EM / EX / BR	EM / EX / BR	EM / EX / BR	EM / EX / BR	EM / EX / BR
	EM / EX / BR	EM / EX / BR	EM / EX / BR	EM / EX / BR	EM / EX / BR
	EM / EX / BR	EM / EX / BR	EM / EX / BR	EM / EX / BR	EM / EX / BR

ELD Standards Record Sheet

Teacher: _____ **Class:** _____

Standards: *PII.A.2*

Guided Activities and Proficiency Levels:

Students:	#1	#2	#3	#4	#5
	EM / EX / BR	EM / EX / BR	EM / EX / BR	EM / EX / BR	EM / EX / BR
	EM / EX / BR	EM / EX / BR	EM / EX / BR	EM / EX / BR	EM / EX / BR
	EM / EX / BR	EM / EX / BR	EM / EX / BR	EM / EX / BR	EM / EX / BR
	EM / EX / BR	EM / EX / BR	EM / EX / BR	EM / EX / BR	EM / EX / BR
	EM / EX / BR	EM / EX / BR	EM / EX / BR	EM / EX / BR	EM / EX / BR
	EM / EX / BR	EM / EX / BR	EM / EX / BR	EM / EX / BR	EM / EX / BR
	EM / EX / BR	EM / EX / BR	EM / EX / BR	EM / EX / BR	EM / EX / BR
	EM / EX / BR	EM / EX / BR	EM / EX / BR	EM / EX / BR	EM / EX / BR
	EM / EX / BR	EM / EX / BR	EM / EX / BR	EM / EX / BR	EM / EX / BR
	EM / EX / BR	EM / EX / BR	EM / EX / BR	EM / EX / BR	EM / EX / BR
	EM / EX / BR	EM / EX / BR	EM / EX / BR	EM / EX / BR	EM / EX / BR
	EM / EX / BR	EM / EX / BR	EM / EX / BR	EM / EX / BR	EM / EX / BR
	EM / EX / BR	EM / EX / BR	EM / EX / BR	EM / EX / BR	EM / EX / BR
	EM / EX / BR	EM / EX / BR	EM / EX / BR	EM / EX / BR	EM / EX / BR
	EM / EX / BR	EM / EX / BR	EM / EX / BR	EM / EX / BR	EM / EX / BR
	EM / EX / BR	EM / EX / BR	EM / EX / BR	EM / EX / BR	EM / EX / BR
	EM / EX / BR	EM / EX / BR	EM / EX / BR	EM / EX / BR	EM / EX / BR
	EM / EX / BR	EM / EX / BR	EM / EX / BR	EM / EX / BR	EM / EX / BR
	EM / EX / BR	EM / EX / BR	EM / EX / BR	EM / EX / BR	EM / EX / BR
	EM / EX / BR	EM / EX / BR	EM / EX / BR	EM / EX / BR	EM / EX / BR

Practice Activity #1

Name: ···

Directions:

1: Practice reading the text aloud:

☐ To myself   ☐ With a partner   ☐ With an adult

2: Use the text to complete the graphic organizer (*words, phrases, pictures*)

Computers

(1) Have you used a computer? More than likely you use a computer every day. Computers are electronic devices that store and process data, or information, very quickly. People use computers in many different ways.

(2) One way computers are used is to complete work. Computers help people type, store, and send all kinds of information. Students in school can use a computer to type their essays or put together a math powerpoint presentation.

(3) A second way computers are used is for communication. People can talk to others using a computer through installed microphones, cameras, and software. People can talk to others anywhere in the world!

(4) A third way that people use computers is for fun. Some people play games on it. Others use it to draw and create things.

(5) Computers have revolutionized, or changed, the way we live.

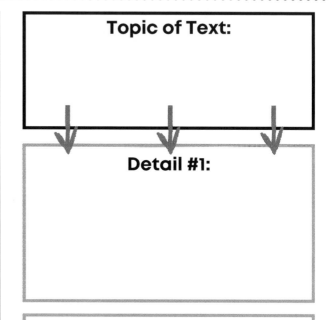

Topic of Text:

Detail #1:

Detail #2:

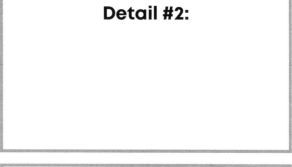

Detail #3:

Practice Activity #1

Name: ....

Directions: Use the text and graphic organizer to answer the questions.

1 What is the main idea of the text?

    A. games

    B. computers

    C. people

2 Which picture shows a computer?

A	B	C

3 What does the word data mean?

    A. computer

    B. electronic device

    C. information

4 How have computers revolutionized, or changed, the way we live?

....

....

Practice Activity #2

Name: ....

Directions:

1: Practice reading the text aloud:

☐ To myself   ☐ With a partner   ☐ With an adult

2: Use the text to complete the graphic organizer (*words, phrases, pictures*)

Sports

(1) There are many different kinds of sports. Sports are active activities in which individuals or teams compete. Participating in sports is a great way to build confidence and sportsmanship.

(2) One popular type of sport is basketball. Basketball is a team sport. People work together to throw a basketball into a basket. The team with the most points wins.

(3) A second popular sport is track. For track, people run on a field. They compete with others. The person who crosses the finish line first is the winner.

(4) A third popular sport is soccer. Teams use only their feet to kick and maneuver, or move, a soccer ball down a field. Teams score goals to win.

(5) Participating in sports is a good way to stay active and healthy. It takes practice and skills in order to become better at a sport. People can play as many sports as they like!

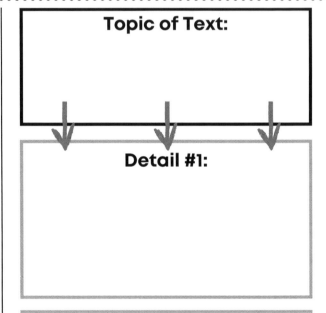

Topic of Text:

Detail #1:

Detail #2:

Detail #3:

128

Practice Activity #2

Name: ....

Directions: Use the text and graphic organizer to answer the questions.

1 What is the main idea of the text?

  A. sports

  B. basketball

  C. school

2 Which picture shows one type of sport?

A   B   C

3 How does a person win in the sport of track?

  A. the last person to cross the finish line

  B. the first person to cross the finish line

  C. the first person to run slow

4 What are some benefits of playing a sport?

....

....

Practice Activity #3

Name: ....

Directions:

1: Practice reading the text aloud:

☐ To myself   ☐ With a partner   ☐ With an adult

2: Use the text to complete the graphic organizer (*words, phrases, pictures*)

Amazon River

(1) The Amazon River is one of the longest rivers in the world. It is located in northern South America. It is one of the world's largest and longest rivers. The river is useful to many people living along it.

(2) Many people living along the Amazon River uses it for travel. The river is used to move people and things from one place along the river to another.

(3) The river is also a source of food for many people. People who live along the river use the water for their crops. People also catch fish from the river for food.

(4) The Amazon River is also an important habitat for animals. Many different animals live in the river, like fish. The largest snake in the world, the anaconda, also lives in the Amazon River. Other animals need the river for drinking water.

(5) The Amazon River is an important part of the environment. It is an intricate, or complicated, water system that needs to be preserved.

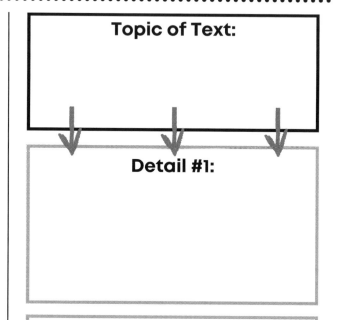

Topic of Text:

Detail #1:

Detail #2:

Detail #3:

130

Practice Activity #3

Name: ....

Directions: Use the text and graphic organizer to answer the questions.

| 1 | **What is the main idea of the text?** |

       A. travel

       B. the Amazon River

       C. South America

| 2 | **Which picture shows one use of the Amazon River?** |

    A   **B**   **C**

| 3 | **How do animals use the river?** |

       A. for growing crops

       B. for drinking water

       C. for cool showers

| 4 | **What are some other ways people use the Amazon River?** |

_____

....

_____

....

_____

Practice Activity #4

Name: ....

Directions:

1: Practice reading the text aloud:
☐ To myself   ☐ With a partner   ☐ With an adult

2: Use the text to complete the graphic organizer (*words, phrases, pictures*)

Walt Disney

(1) Have you ever been to Disneyland? Have you ever seen a classic Disney movie? The man who started it all was Walt Disney.

(2) Walt Disney was a film maker, artist, and business man. He was born on December 5, 1901.

(3) The most famous cartoon character that he created was Mickey Mouse. Many children grew up watching Mickey Mouse cartoons. Other well-known characters soon followed, such as Goofy and Donald Duck.

(4) In the 1950s, Walt Disney created Disneyland in California. It is a theme park where Walt Disney's vision and creativity came alive. There are a lot of fun themed rides and other things to do there.

(5) There are many Disney theme parks around the world now, such as Paris and China. It is a great place for kids and families to spend quality time together. Walt Disney had a big imagination and talent. He dared to dream big and make it a reality.

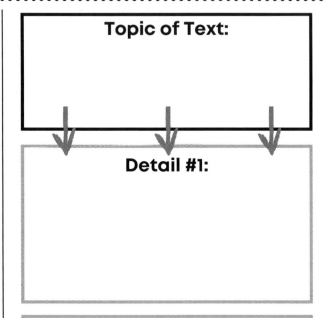

Topic of Text:

Detail #1:

Detail #2:

Detail #3:

132

Reading: *Read an Informational Passage*

Practice Activity #4

Name:

Directions: Use the text and graphic organizer to answer the questions.

1 **What is the main idea of the text?**

A. Mickey Mouse

B. Walt Disney

C. theme parks

2 **Which picture shows a theme park?**

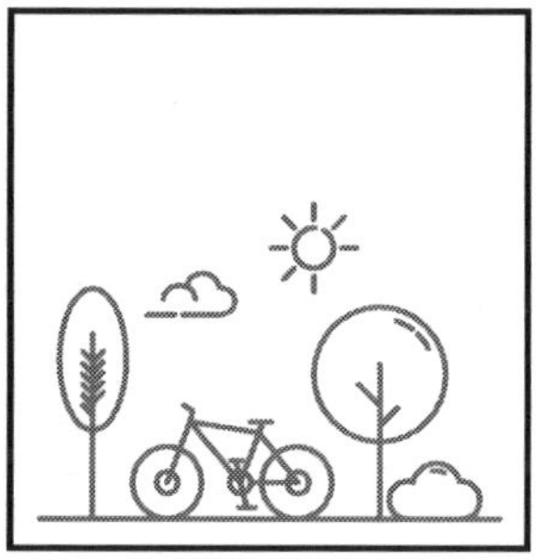

A

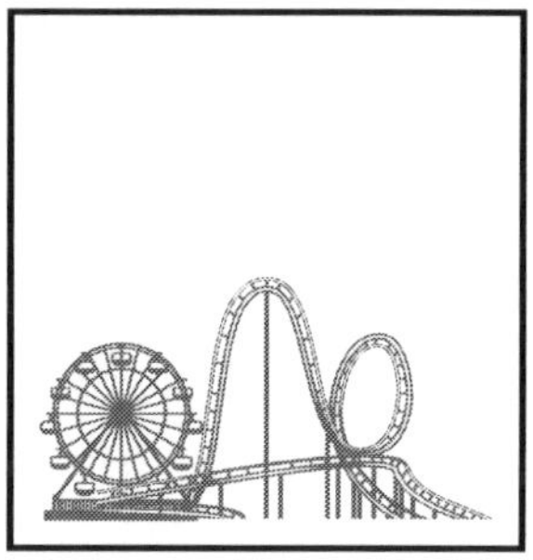

B

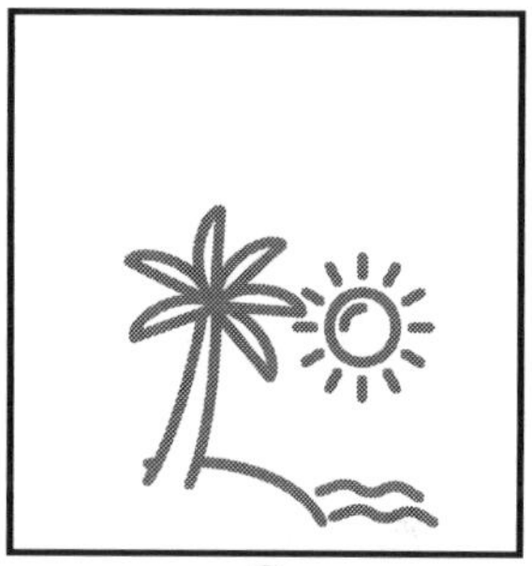

C

3 **Who was Walt Disney?**

A. a chef

B. a teacher

C. a film maker

4 **What is Disneyland?**

Practice Activity #5

Name:

Directions:

1: Practice reading the text aloud:
  ☐ To myself   ☐ With a partner   ☐ With an adult

2: Use the text to complete the graphic organizer (*words, phrases, pictures*)

The South Pole

(1) Most people think more of the North Pole and Santa Claus. However, there is also the South Pole which is located on Antarctica. It is the southern most point on the Earth.

(2) It is extremely cold in the South Pole. The temperature is very harsh and there is a lot of snow and ice. Technically, the South Pole is considered a desert because it does not rain or snow a lot there. Any snow that does fall does not melt. Instead, it continues to build up in layers called ice sheets. There are also glaciers and icebergs in Antarctica.

(3) There are no plants or animals at the South Pole. They can not survive in such a harsh place.

(4) Surprisingly, there are people who live in the South Pole. These people live at a research station. They study many different things about our planet and space at the South Pole. There is an actual pole to mark the South Pole. It is moved every year because the ice moves.

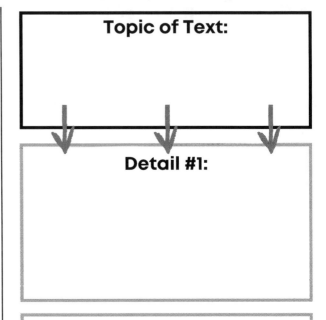

Topic of Text:

Detail #1:

Detail #2:

Detail #3:

Reading: *Read an Informational Passage*

Practice Activity #5

Name: ______________________

Directions: Use the text and graphic organizer to answer the questions.

1 **What is the main idea of the text?**

A. the North Pole

B. ice and snow

C. the South Pole

2 **Which picture shows what the South Pole looks like?**

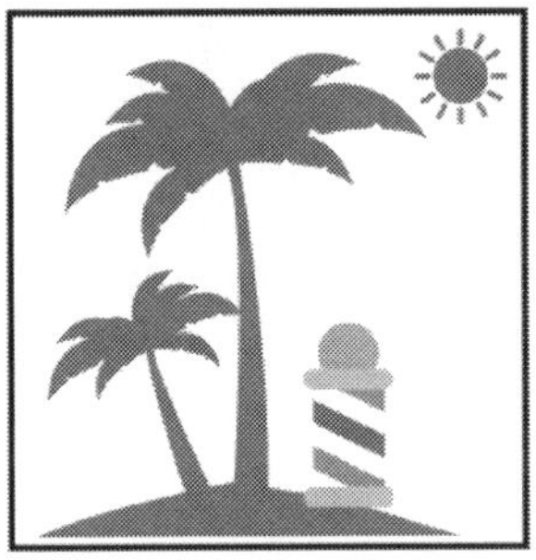

A

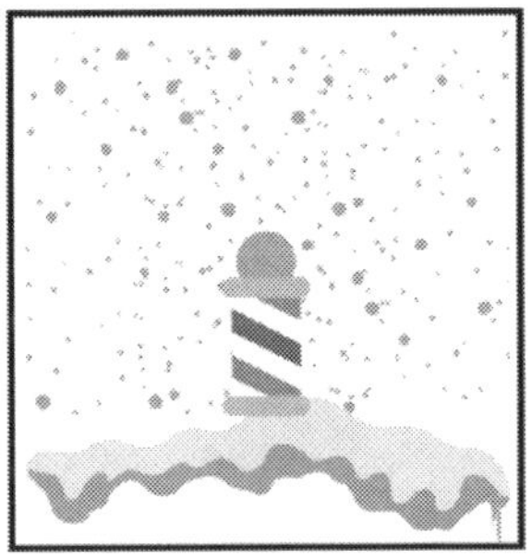

B

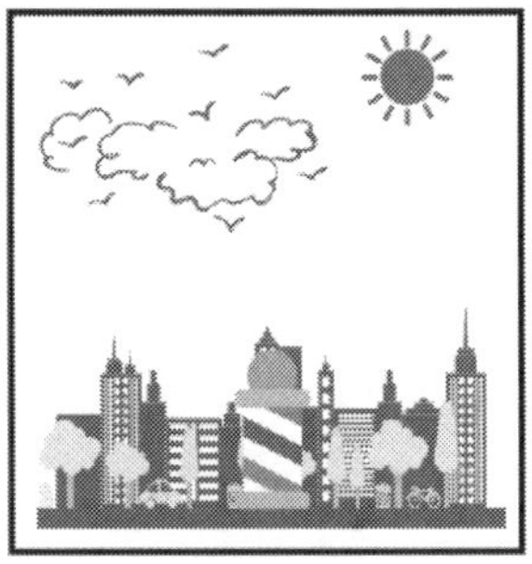

C

3 **Why are there people living at the South Pole?**

A. they are studying many things about Earth

B. they are building big cities

C. they are on vacation

4 **Why is the South Pole considered a desert?**

____

____

THIS PAGE INTENTIONALLY LEFT BLANK

Made in the USA
Las Vegas, NV
26 September 2024

95828096R00079